TEAM

LIGHTHOUSES OF THE WORLD

intra

Visio Series

Cover photo: Kevin Brine, *Peggy's Point Lighthouse*.

Edizioni Intra®
www.intraedizioni.it
info@intra.pro

ISBN 979-12-5991-726-3

Table of Contents

Introduction

What could be more solid, still, and solitary than a lighthouse? And yet, what could be more symbolic, poetic, and evocative?

A lighthouse is stone and light. Architecture and function. But also story, metaphor, hope. It's a technical object charged with emotion—a tool designed for navigation that has, for centuries, also guided the imagination. Whether it's the Lantern of Genoa or the Lighthouse of Alexandria, the beam that cuts across the Atlantic at Fastnet or the sunken ruins at Leptis Magna, every lighthouse is a vertical story that starts on land and reaches toward the sea.

Lighthouses are built to be seen. Not to be inhabited, or visited, or venerated: they are meant to be spotted from afar, to send out a signal that pierces through darkness and fog, to point the way.

That's why, over time, lighthouses have become immensely powerful symbols—in literature, in painting, in photography, and of course in cinema. Think of Proust, Virginia Woolf, Borges, or Prévert, and it becomes clear how the lighthouse has entered Western cultural memory as an icon of solitude and hope, of endurance and doubt. It is a symbol of the one who watches, and also of the one being watched. A sentinel, and at the same time, a boundary.

In both religious and philosophical symbolism, the lighthouse represents guidance, protection, and the watchful gaze of a higher presence that illuminates the path. Its intermittent beam is often used allegorically to represent the fragility of our choices—or the sudden illumination that rescues us from shipwreck. Its architecture is typically simple, vertical, essential. And yet each lighthouse is different: in location, in materials, in era, in fate. Some still stand firm against time and tide; others have succumbed, swallowed by the sea or replaced by technology. But even those—forgotten, dismantled, vanished—deserve remembrance. Because every lighthouse is also a vessel of history.

This book gathers fifty lighthouses, selected with care and passion. It is not a census, nor an atlas—it is a visual and narrative journey, like all volumes in the Visio Series by Edizioni Intra. A journey through images, words, and QR codes that let you see, listen, and explore. The experience is immersive, the geographic leap constant: from Egypt to the United States, from Scandinavia to Italy, from the cliffs of Wales to the Mediterranean.

We admit, the selection wasn't easy. We included famous lighthouses and lesser-known ones, working lights and vanished ones, Eastern and Western, continental and island-based. Some are now tourist destinations, others remain remote and unreachable. But all of them, without exception, possess a narrative power of their own—whether because of their shape, their location, the history they bear, or the photographs that made them iconic.

We deliberately chose not to divide the book into "past" and "present" lighthouses. Alphabetical order—and the uniqueness of each architectural gesture—seemed more honest, more true to our purpose. Which is not to classify, but to tell stories.

This is not an exhaustive volume—no book of this kind ever could be. But every lighthouse included here speaks of something far greater than itself: it tells the story of a world. Or at least, it lights one up.

Enjoy the read—and safe travels among the lights of the world.

READING NOTES

To enhance the reading experience and make it more immersive, this book includes QR codes that provide instant access to external digital content. A QR code is a two-dimensional barcode that, when scanned using the camera on a smartphone, tablet, or computer, automatically opens a link.

For each lighthouse entry, you'll find several main QR codes:

Google Maps: to explore the exact geographic location of the structure, view it from above, and, when available, activate Street View for a virtual outdoor tour.

Google Earth: to observe the structure in three dimensions, contextualize it within its urban or natural environment, and appreciate its visual and architectural impact from a global, immersive perspective.

YouTube: to watch videos and documentaries providing further insight into the site.

Below each QR code is only the logo of the platform it links to, ensuring a clean, fast, and visually streamlined experience

To use this feature properly:
1. Open your device's camera and point it at the QR code.
2. If your device supports automatic QR code reading, a clickable link will appear.
3. Alternatively, you can use a free QR code reader app, easily available in all major app stores.

LIGHTHOUSES OF THE WORLD

Australia – Cape Byron Lighthouse

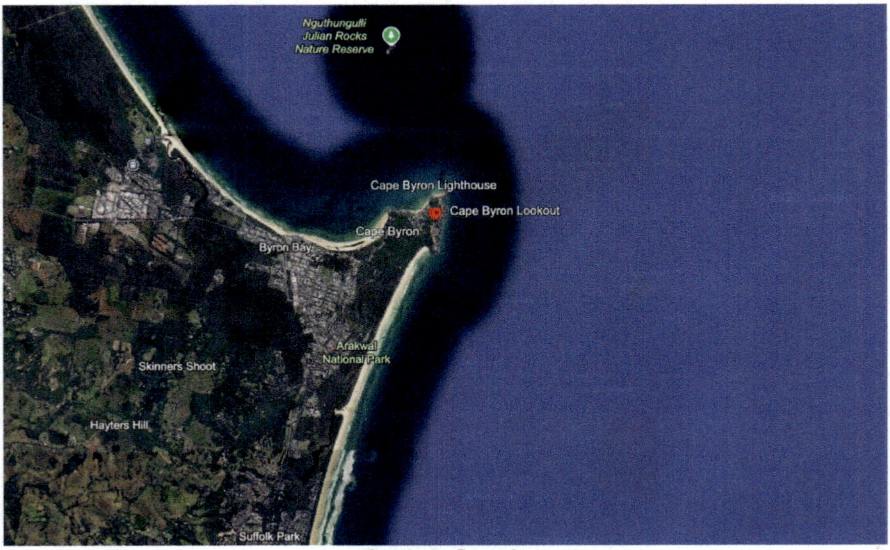

Source: Google

Cape Byron Lighthouse – Photo: BigTo/Wikimedia

Lighthouse Name	Cape Byron Lighthouse
Location	Byron Bay, Australia
Height	22 m (tower height) – 94 m a.s.l. (focal height)
Year Built	1901
Range	27 nautical miles (approx. 50 km)
Type	First-order rotating optic lighthouse
Key Features	Easternmost lighthouse on mainland Australia
Accessibility	Open to the public – guided tours and interpretive center available

Lighthouse Rd, Byron Bay
NSW 2481, Australia

9J6P+JF Byron Bay, NSW,
Australia

Cape Byron Lighthouse
Videos and documentaries

At the easternmost point of mainland Australia, where the first rays of dawn touch the continent, stands the Cape Byron Lighthouse—a white stone sentinel that has watched over the Pacific Ocean for more than a century. Built in 1901 atop the cliffs of Byron Bay, this lighthouse is not only a navigational landmark but also a symbol of Australia's natural beauty and coastal heritage.

The project was commissioned to Charles Harding, and the 22-meter-high tower was constructed in white concrete in a classical style, with its central lantern positioned 94 meters above sea level. At the time of its construction, Cape Byron housed the most powerful first-order lens optic in the country, visible up to 27 nautical miles. Originally fueled by kerosene, the light is now fully automated and electrically powered, though the original structure remains unchanged.

Today, the lighthouse is one of the most beloved attractions in New South Wales. Tens of thousands of visitors make the hike each year from the center of Byron Bay to its base, passing through nature reserves, coastal forests, and breathtaking viewpoints. From the top, one can observe the meeting of ocean currents, migrating whales, and—on especially clear days—even the curvature of the Earth. The lighthouse is open to the public, features an interpretive center focused on Australian maritime history and local communities, and is operated by the Australian Maritime Safety Authority.

Cape Byron has become a symbol of light and memory—a place where geography becomes poetry, and where each night the lantern breathes life into the vastness of the sea.

Photo: 2017, Bigballsybananas/Wikimedia

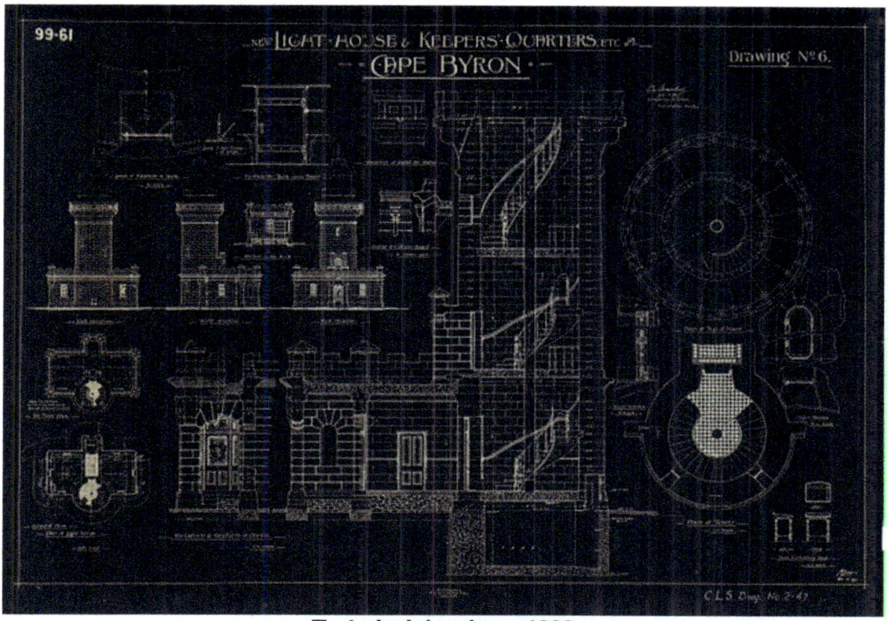

Technical drawings, 1899

Photo: 2007, JWarnes/Wikimedia

Brazil – Barra Lighthouse

Source: Google

Photo: 2017, Mirella856/Wikimedia

Lighthouse Name	Farol da Barra
Location	Salvador, Brazil
Height	22 m (tower height) – 37 m a.s.l. (focal height)
Year Built	1698 (rebuilt in 1839)
Range	18 nautical miles (approx. 33 km)
Type	Rotating light lighthouse with modern optics on a historic structure
Key Features	One of the oldest active lighthouses in the Americas
Accessibility	Open to the public – home to the Nautical Museum of Bahia

Barra, Salvador - Bahia, Brazil

XFQ8+WR Barra, Salvador - Bahia, Brazil

Barra Lighthouse Videos and documentaries

Located at the entrance to the Bay of All Saints in the city of Salvador, the Farol da Barra is one of the oldest and most iconic maritime landmarks in Brazil. Originally built in 1698 atop the ruins of the Santo Antônio da Barra Fort, it was among the first lighthouses constructed in the Americas. The current structure dates back to 1839, featuring a cylindrical tower with distinctive black and white stripes, standing 72 feet (22 meters) tall and elegantly overlooking the coastline.

The lighthouse marks the entrance to one of South America's most important natural harbors and served for centuries as a key reference point for both commercial and military navigation. Its beam reaches over 20 miles (approximately 33 kilometers) out to sea, and its position on a rocky promontory offers sweeping views of the Atlantic Ocean.

Today, the Farol da Barra is beautifully preserved and houses the Nautical Museum of Bahia, which tells the maritime history of the region through archaeological artifacts, navigation instruments, and historical maps. From the panoramic terrace atop the lighthouse, visitors enjoy breathtaking views of Salvador's coastline—especially striking at sunset, when golden light bathes the tower and surrounding waters.

A symbol of resilience, memory, and beauty, the Farol da Barra is much more than a beacon: it's a meeting point of colonial history, military architecture, and tropical landscape. Every night, as its light shines across the sea, it continues a legacy that has guided sailors for more than three centuries.

Photo: 2022, Milena Cintra/Wikimedia

Canada – Fisgard Lighthouse

Photo: David Broad/Wikimedia

Photo: Sarena D/Wikimedia

Lighthouse Name	Fisgard Lighthouse
Location	Colwood (Victoria), Canada
Height	14.6 m (tower height) – 21 m a.s.l. (focal height)
Year Built	1860
Range	17 nautical miles (approx. 31 km)
Type	Masonry tower with automated lantern on a historic structure
Key Features	First lighthouse built on Canada's Pacific coast
Accessibility	No longer active – open to the public as a historic site

603 Fort Rodd Hill Rd, Victoria, BC V9C 2W8, Canada

CHJ2+5X Victoria, BC, Canada

Fort Rodd Hill and Fisgard Lighthouse
Videos and documentaries

Rising proudly on the coast of British Columbia, at the entrance to Esquimalt Harbour near the city of Victoria, the Fisgard Lighthouse was built in 1860 and holds the distinction of being the first lighthouse on Canada's Pacific coast. It stands as a testament to the region's growing strategic and commercial significance during the British colonial period.

The 14.6-meter white masonry tower is topped with a red roof and lantern—a striking color contrast set against the dark waters and coniferous forest of the Pacific shoreline. Beside the tower, the restored keeper's house completes an architectural ensemble that appears nearly untouched by time. Originally, the light guided Royal Navy vessels and merchant ships heading toward Esquimalt, then an imperial naval base. The lighthouse was constructed using materials brought up from San Francisco and operated for decades by lighthouse keepers and their families—isolated yet vital to maritime safety.

Today, though the lantern has been automated and is no longer in use as a navigational aid, the lighthouse is open to the public as part of the Fort Rodd Hill National Historic Site. Visitors can explore the interior, climb toward the lantern, view museum exhibits, and enjoy spectacular views of the ocean and the nearby American coastline. Fisgard is no longer a functioning beacon, but it remains a place where history, landscape, and colonial memory converge. A symbol of Canada's maritime past, it continues—figuratively—to shine light on the story of a nation facing the vast Pacific.

Photo: Darren Kirby/Wikimedia

Canada – Peggy’s Point Lighthouse

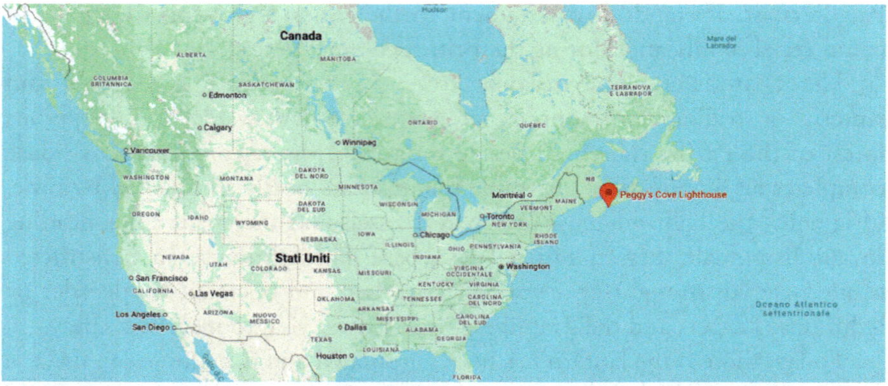

Source: Google

Photo: 2008, Taxiarchos228/Wikimedia

Lighthouse Name	Peggy's Point Lighthouse
Location	Peggy's Cove, Canada
Height	15 m (tower height) – 22 m a.s.l. (focal height)
Year Built	1915
Range	10 nautical miles (approx. 18.5 km)
Type	Automated lighthouse with modern lamp in a concrete tower
Key Features	One of the most photographed and iconic lighthouses in North America
Accessibility	Interior not accessible – viewable from outside

Peggys Point Rd, Peggy's Cove, NS B3Z 3S1, Canada

F3RJ+MG Peggys Cove, NS, Canada

Peggy's Point Lighthouse Videos and documentaries

Set among the granite rocks carved by Atlantic winds and ancient glaciers, Peggy's Point Lighthouse is arguably the most famous lighthouse in Canada. Its white silhouette topped with a red lantern, perched on a rocky outcrop overlooking the ocean, has become a national symbol—immortalized in postcards, paintings, and photographs from travelers around the world.

Built in 1915 to replace an earlier wooden structure, the lighthouse was constructed in reinforced concrete with a distinctive hexagonal base that stands sharply against the sky of Nova Scotia. At 15 meters tall, its beam still guides vessels toward the entrance of St. Margaret's Bay—though today its role is more symbolic than practical.

Peggy's Cove is a fishing village that has preserved the rugged charm of the North Atlantic: high-hulled boats, weathered wooden houses, and rocks battered by the sea. The area draws large numbers of tourists, but the lighthouse itself remains closed to the public for safety reasons. Visitors can, however, walk among the rocks, listen to the crashing waves, and admire the lighthouse as a silent sentinel between ocean and sky.

Peggy's Point is also the subject of local legend: according to the most famous version, a young shipwreck survivor named Peggy washed ashore here and gave her name to the bay. Whether true or not, the lighthouse remains a poetic presence—a light in the fog, telling stories without uttering a word.

Photo: 2017, Shawn M. Kent/Wikimedia

Denmark – Rubjerg Knude Fyr

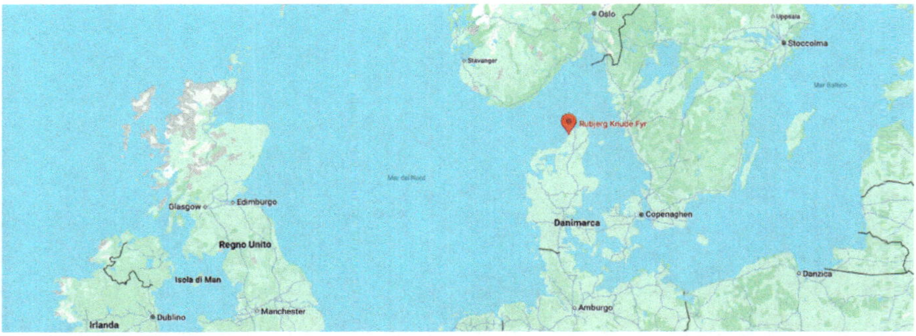

Source: Google

Photo: Ansgar Koreng/Wikimedia

Lighthouse Name	Rubjerg Knude Fyr
Location	Lønstrup, Denmark
Height	23 m
Year Built	1900
Range	N/A (deactivated in 1968)
Type	Brick tower on sandy dune – originally kerosene-lit, later electrified
Key Features	Historic lighthouse threatened by coastal erosion and relocated in 2019
Accessibility	No longer active – accessible to the public as a scenic viewpoint

Fyrvejen 110, 9480 Løkken, Denmark

CQXG+J5 Løkken, Denmark

Rubjerg Knude Fyr Videos and documentaries

Amid the shifting dunes and fierce winds of Denmark's northern Jutland coast, Rubjerg Knude Fyr stands like a relic of sand and time. Built in 1900 on a 60-meter-high cliff overlooking the North Sea, the lighthouse battled for decades against the unstoppable advance of nature: it was buried by drifting sand, threatened by marine erosion, and eventually faced an uncertain fate.

The 23-meter brick tower was originally equipped with a kerosene lantern, later converted to electric light, but it was decommissioned in 1968—not due to technical obsolescence, but because the encroaching dune had made the light completely invisible. Around it, the keeper's buildings were abandoned and gradually swallowed by the sandy landscape.

Having become a symbol of both fragility and resilience, Rubjerg Knude Fyr was the focus of a dramatic engineering rescue in 2019: the entire tower was moved 70 meters inland on rails to prevent its imminent collapse. The operation captured international media attention and gave new life to the lighthouse, now a scenic overlook and tourist destination.

Today, those who climb to the top are rewarded with breathtaking views of the gray waves of the North Sea and the ever-changing Danish heathland beneath an equally changeable sky. Rubjerg Knude no longer shines its beam, but it has become a beacon of awareness—of nature's power, of time's transformations, and of the urgent need to preserve what might otherwise disappear.

Photo: ClausNe/Wikimedia

Egypt – Lighthouse of Alexandria

Source: Google

Lighthouse Name	Lighthouse of Alexandria
Location	Pharos Island, Alexandria, Egypt
Height	Approximately 110–130 m (ancient estimates)
Year Built	Construction completed around 280 BCE
Range	Estimated visibility: up to 50 km
Type	Three-tiered structure (square base, octagonal body, cylindrical top)
Key Features	One of the Seven Wonders of the Ancient World – symbol of ancient navigation
Accessibility	No longer exists – collapsed between the 13th and 14th centuries due to earthquakes; ruins submerged

As Sayalah Sharq, Al Gomrok, Alexandria 5321431, Egypt

6V7P+F5 Al Gomrok, Egypt

Lighthouse of Alexandria Videos and documentaries

In the heart of the eastern Mediterranean, where Egypt opens to the open sea, once stood the most legendary lighthouse of all: the Pharos of Alexandria. Its light, lit over 2,200 years ago, was the first to become a symbol of knowledge, technology, and naval power—earning its place among the Seven Wonders of the Ancient World. Commissioned by Ptolemy I Soter and completed under Ptolemy II Philadelphus around 280 BCE, the lighthouse was built on the island of Pharos, connected to the mainland by a long causeway known as the Heptastadion. The tower, made of limestone and estimated to be between 110 and 130 meters tall according to ancient sources, towered over the port and the entire Hellenistic city of Alexandria, then one of the world's major centers of culture. Its architecture was grand and complex: a square base, an octagonal middle section, and a cylindrical top, where a fire burned both day and night. A sophisticated system of polished bronze mirrors reflected the flame, making it visible up to 50 kilometers away. According to some Arab historians, the lighthouse even employed lenses—centuries ahead of modern optical science.

The Pharos stood for over a millennium before being destroyed by a series of powerful earthquakes between the 13th and 14th centuries. Its stones were later used to build the Qaitbay Fortress (15th century), which now stands on the same promontory. Other fragments remain submerged in the harbor of Alexandria, the focus of underwater archaeological research.

The Lighthouse of Alexandria was not merely a beacon—it was the forerunner of all modern lighthouses: the founding light of organized navigation, of science applied to orientation, of humanity's eternal effort to understand the sea. Even today, the word for "lighthouse" in many languages derives from Pharos, a testament to its enduring legacy.

Image (reconstruction): 2021, Віщун/Wikimedia

Finland – Märket Lighthouse

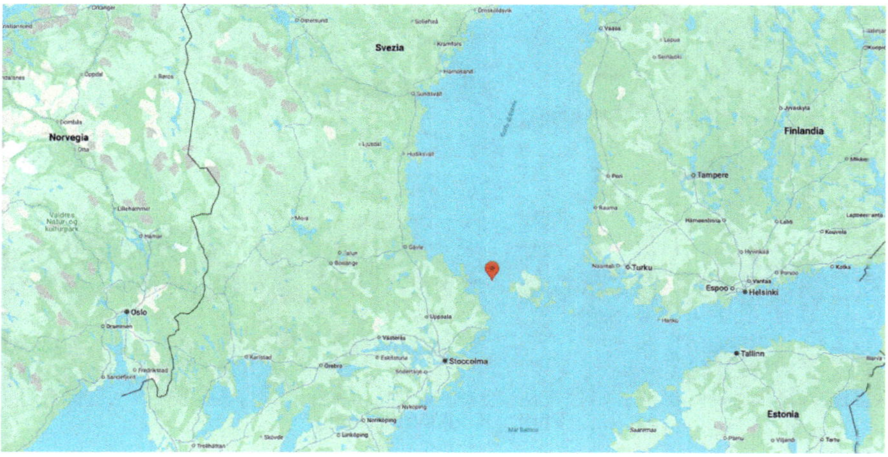

Source: Google

Photo: 2009, Islander/Wikimedia

Photo: Koski/Wikimedia

Lighthouse Name	Märket Lighthouse
Location	Märket Islet, Finland
Height	14.5 m (tower height) – 22.6 m a.s.l. (focal height)
Year Built	1885
Range	11 nautical miles (approx. 20 km)
Type	Red brick tower with octagonal cast-iron lantern
Key Features	Lighthouse built on the border between Finland and Sweden
Accessibility	No longer operational – visitable on special excursions

Märket, Finland

60°18'03"N 19°07'55"E

Märket Lighthouse
Videos and documentaries

In the heart of the Baltic Sea, on a windswept islet barely rising above the waves, stands Märket Lighthouse—a solitary and captivating beacon built in one of the world's most peculiar border zones. Märket is divided between Finland and Sweden, and although the lighthouse was built by the Finns in 1885, it was accidentally placed on Swedish territory—an anomaly that was later "corrected" with a curious border adjustment now visible on maps as a Z-shaped kink.

The 14.5-meter red brick tower is topped with an octagonal cast-iron lantern that once projected its beam 11 nautical miles across the sea. But more than the light itself, it is the story behind Märket that makes the place remarkable. Isolated, treeless, and inhabited only by seabirds and wind, the lighthouse was manned by keepers for nearly a century, under harsh and extreme conditions.

Automated in 1979 and fully decommissioned in 2007, the lighthouse has since been partially restored thanks to the dedication of a Finnish volunteer group. Today, it can be visited on rare occasions through boat excursions—weather permitting.

Märket has also gained fame among amateur radio operators around the world, who compete for the chance to broadcast from the lighthouse, located in one of the rarest DX entities. Yet beyond the technical feats, what truly resonates is the feeling of standing at the edge of the world, in a place where geography becomes narrative, and light has given way to memory.

France – La Jument Lighthouse

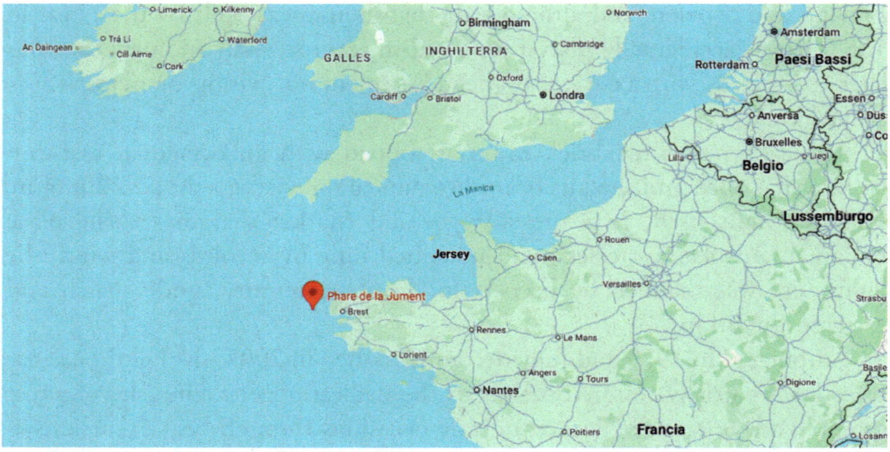

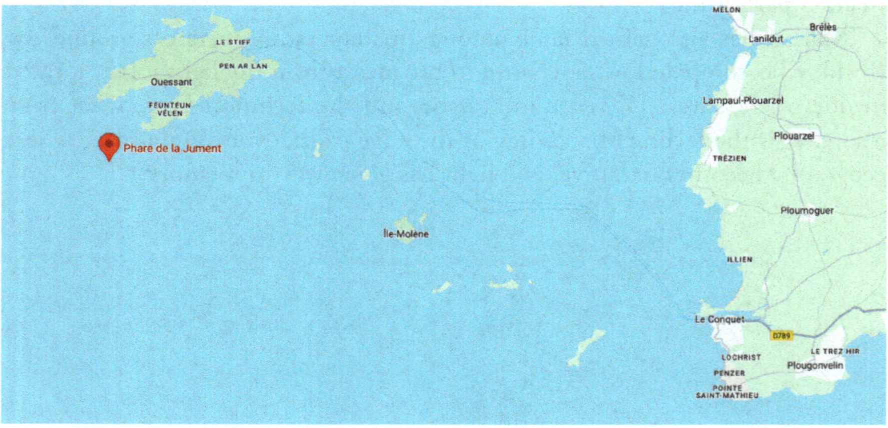

Map source: Google – Photo: 2003, Flore Allemandou/Wikimedia

Lighthouse Name	La Jument
Location	Off the coast of Ushant (Ouessant), Brittany, France
Height	48 m (tower height) – 37 m a.s.l. (focal height)
Year Built	1911
Range	22 nautical miles (approx. 41 km)
Type	Cylindrical red granite tower – automatic light
Key Features	Offshore lighthouse made famous by Jean Guichard's photographs
Accessibility	Not accessible – visible only by sea or helicopter

Ushant, France

CVF8+98 Ouessant, France

La Jument
Videos and documentaries

In the heart of the Atlantic, off the stormy coasts of Brittany, stands La Jument Lighthouse—an heroic sentinel and one of the most iconic and captivating structures in maritime history. Its name—La Jument ("the mare")—comes from a dangerous submerged rock that for centuries claimed countless ships passing near the island of Ushant (Ouessant).

Built under extreme conditions and completed in 1911, the lighthouse stands fully offshore, where waves can reach up to 30 meters and crash violently against the tower. The project was initiated after a particularly tragic shipwreck in 1888, which prompted a shipowner to partially fund the construction. La Jument was one of the first offshore lighthouses to be built without access to dry land for most of the day—a remarkable engineering feat for its time.

But La Jument owes its worldwide fame to an iconic moment: a photograph taken in 1989 by Jean Guichard, showing a colossal wave engulfing the lighthouse just as the keeper opens the door—unaware that the photographer is approaching by helicopter. That image traveled the world and became the ultimate symbol of man's struggle against the sea.

Today, the lighthouse is fully automated and no longer inhabited. Its beam still reaches 22 nautical miles, watching over one of the most treacherous stretches of the Atlantic coast. While it cannot be visited, it can be glimpsed from the sea—or immortalized in posters, books, and collective memory.

La Jument is more than just a lighthouse: it is an epic icon, a monument to human endurance against the fury of nature. A lighthouse one never forgets.

Photo: 2007, Falken/Wikimedia

France – Phare d’Ar-Men

Source: Google

Photo: 2020, Gzen92/Wikimedia

Lighthouse Name	Phare d'Ar-Men
Location	Off the coast of Île de Sein, Brittany, France
Height	32 m (tower height) – 37 m a.s.l. (focal height)
Year Built	1881 (construction began in 1867)
Range	23 nautical miles (approx. 43 km)
Type	Granite tower built on isolated rock – rotating optic
Key Features	One of the most difficult and isolated lighthouses ever built
Accessibility	Not accessible – visible only from the sea

22X2+W7 Île-de-Sein, France

22X2+W7 Île-de-Sein, France

Phare d'Ar-Men
Videos and documentaries

In the Atlantic Ocean, where the waters grow darker and storms are the rule rather than the exception, stands one of the world's most legendary and inaccessible lighthouses: the Phare d'Ar-Men. Built on a tiny rock off the Île de Sein at the far western tip of Brittany, it is the ultimate symbol of isolation, courage, and human endurance in the face of the sea's fury.

Construction began in 1867, but the extreme location and nearly impossible access meant that only seven stone blocks were laid in the first year. It took 14 years to complete the towering granite structure, which rises 32 meters above the wave-battered reef. The light was first lit in 1881, and from then on it became one of the harshest posts for lighthouse keepers: months-long shifts, complete solitude, and storms that often made any contact with the mainland impossible. "Ar-Men" means "the rock" in Breton—an apt and powerful name. The lighthouse could only be reached in perilous conditions, often using a suspended cage system between boat and tower when the sea allowed. The stories and diaries left behind by its keepers describe a life of wind, reading, silence, and storms.

Automated in 1990, the Phare d'Ar-Men is no longer accessible and remains isolated in the middle of the ocean. Yet its slender silhouette—painted in black and white with its name clearly marked at the base—continues to serve as a reference point for sailors and a cultural icon for the people of Brittany. More than just a lighthouse, it is a stone legend. A place that embodies the extreme: of geography, of duty, and of the human spirit.

Photo: 2011, Jocelyn Caron/Wikimedia

France – Phare de Cordouan

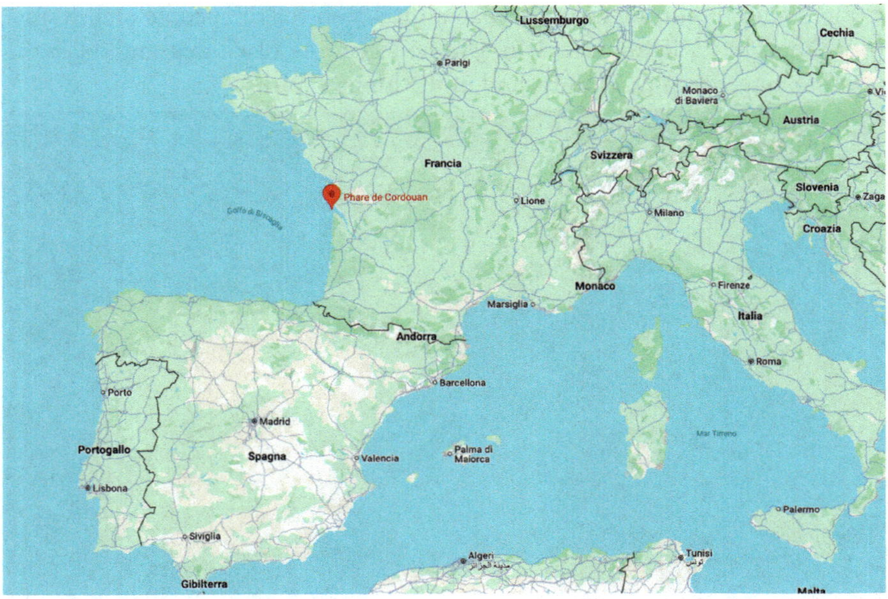

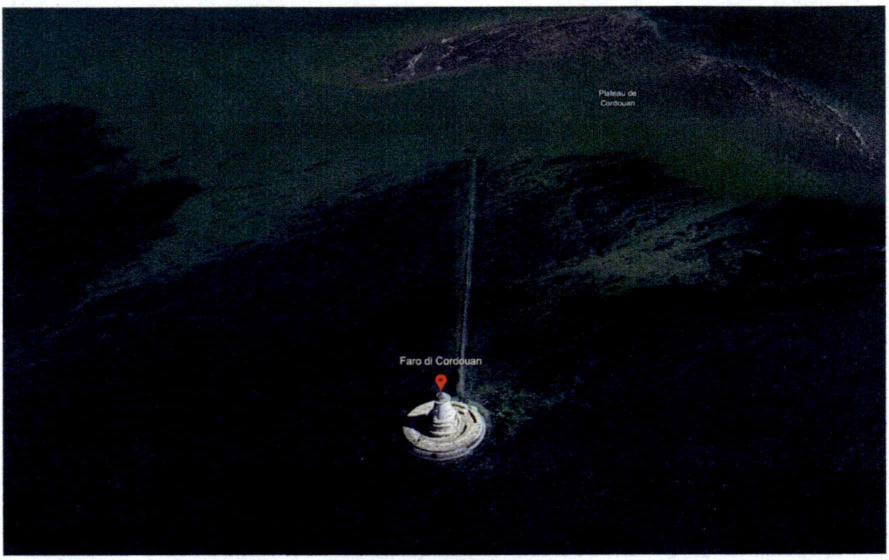

Source: Google

Lighthouse Name	Phare de Cordouan
Location	Gironde Estuary, Nouvelle-Aquitaine, France
Height	67.5 m
Year Built	1611 (current; origin in the 14th century)
Range	22 nautical miles (approx. 41 km)
Type	White stone tower – Renaissance and Classical architecture, modernized optic
Key Features	Oldest monumental lighthouse in France still in service – UNESCO World Heritage Site
Accessibility	Open to the public – reachable by boat, visitable at set times and conditions

33123 Le Verdon-sur-Mer, France

HFPG+HQ Le Verdon-sur-Mer, France

Phare de Cordouan Videos and documentaries

Standing for over four centuries, isolated in the Atlantic Ocean and accessible only at low tide or by boat, the Phare de Cordouan is more than a lighthouse: it is a palace at sea, a royal monument to light and science.

Located at the mouth of the Gironde estuary, facing Royan and Le Verdon-sur-Mer, it was built between 1584 and 1611 by order of Henry III and later Henry IV, replacing an earlier medieval tower from the 14th century. Designed by Louis de Foix, it is a true example of Renaissance architecture applied to a coastal structure, complete with vaulted ceilings, monumental staircases, sculpted decorations, and even a Baroque-style chapel inside.

Climbing its 301 stone steps is like walking through the centuries of maritime history. At 67.5 meters tall, Cordouan is now fully automated and in perfect working order, and it is considered the oldest offshore lighthouse in the world still in operation.

In 2021, it was inscribed on the UNESCO World Heritage list as an "exceptional example of a monumental lighthouse" and a technical-artistic masterpiece. For the French, it is "le roi des phares"—the king of lighthouses: a beacon that blends beauty, utility, resilience, and history, and one that every traveler dreams of visiting at least once.

Photo: 2012, Dimimis/Wikimedia

France – Phare du Créac'h

Source: Google

Photo: 2016, Denis Schwartz/Wikimedia

Photo: Folork/Wikimedia

Lighthouse Name	Phare du Créac'h
Location	Île d'Ouessant, France
Height	54.8 m (tower height) – 70 m a.s.l. (focal height)
Year Built	1863
Range	32 nautical miles (approx. 59 km)
Type	Black and white stone tower with rotating optic and halogen lamps
Key Features	One of the most powerful lighthouses in the world – symbol of Brittany
Accessibility	Not accessible – adjacent museum open to the public

Créac'h, Le Créac'h, 29242 Ouessant, France

FV5C+M9 Ouessant, France

Phare du Créac'h Videos and documentaries

At the far western edge of France, where the Atlantic lashes the coast with primal force, stands the majestic Phare du Créac'h, sentinel of the Île d'Ouessant and one of the most powerful lighthouses in the world. Its beam, visible up to 32 nautical miles, has marked the threshold between land and the vast ocean for generations. Built in 1863 on a rocky rise, the Créac'h is known for its striking black-and-white striped stone tower, which has become a symbol of Breton identity. Nearly 55 meters tall, it is topped with a rotating optic powered by high-intensity halogen lamps, capable of piercing through the fog and storms that plague this stretch of coastline—among the most dangerous in Europe for navigation.

The lighthouse marks the entrance to the English Channel and serves as a beacon for ships bound for the major ports of the north. Though automated, it remains active and operational. It also houses the Musée des Phares et Balises, a maritime signal museum that chronicles the history of French lighthouses through models, optical instruments, chronometers, and firsthand accounts from lighthouse keepers.

The Île d'Ouessant, a wild and wind-battered island, has become almost mythical to sailors, and the Créac'h is its emblem. The tower itself is not open to the public, but the allure of the site speaks for itself: listening to the wind sweeping through the rocks and watching the beam cut through the darkness is enough to feel the poetic power of this remote maritime outpost.

France – Phare du Petit Minou

Source: Google

Photo: 2020, Richard LE GOC/Wikimedia

Lighthouse Name	Phare du Petit Minou
Location	Plouzané (Brest), France
Height	26 m (tower height) – 34 m a.s.l. (focal height)
Year Built	1848
Range	19 nautical miles (approx. 35 km)
Type	Cylindrical masonry tower with rotating optics – red and white light
Key Features	Aligns ships with the safe channel into the Port of Brest
Accessibility	Not open to the public. Coastal path accessible

Pointe du Minou, 29280 Plouzané, France

89PP+MC Plouzané, France

Phare du Petit Minou Videos and documentaries

Perched between rocks and tides, connected to the mainland by an elegant stone bridge, the Phare du Petit Minou is one of the most picturesque lighthouses on the Breton coast. Built in 1848 on a rocky promontory in the town of Plouzané, just a few kilometers from Brest, the lighthouse faces the Atlantic like a gentle yet unyielding guardian of one of France's most strategic naval ports. The cylindrical stone tower, 26 meters tall, projects an alternating red and white beam designed to precisely align ships with the safe channel leading into the Brest roadstead—steering them clear of hidden reefs and treacherous waters. The red light, in particular, warns mariners if they stray from the designated course.

The lighthouse takes its name from the nearby Fort du Petit Minou, built in the 18th century to defend the harbor entrance. Together, the fort and lighthouse form one of Brittany's most iconic images—especially at sunset, when the warm glow of the sun reflects off the stone arch of the bridge and the damp granite of the tower. Although the lighthouse itself is not open to the public, it can be easily reached along the GR34 coastal path, which offers breathtaking views of waves, cliffs, and naval traffic. On stormy days, gusts of wind carry sea spray across the footbridge, making the experience even more intense. More than just a navigational aid, the Petit Minou is a living fragment of France's maritime landscape: a postcard-perfect lighthouse, yes—but also a precise machine, built to protect, to guide, and to tell the story of the sea.

Photo: 2013, Olivier Dugornay/Wikimedia

Germany – Lindau Lighthouse

Source: Google

Photo: 2014, H. Helmlechner/Wikimedia

Lighthouse Name	Lindau Lighthouse
Location	Lindau, Germany
Height	33 m (tower height) – 35 m a.s.l. (focal height)
Year Built	1856
Range	N/A (mainly used for port navigation)
Type	Masonry tower with mechanical clock and directional light
Key Features	Germany's only lighthouse with a clock on its façade, overlooking Lake Constance
Accessibility	Open to the public – visitable during summer months

Hafenpl., 88131 Lindau, Germany

GMVM+5C Lindau, Germany

Lindau
Videos and documentaries

Overlooking the picturesque harbor of Lindau, on the German side of Lake Constance, the Lindau Lighthouse combines architectural elegance with symbolic meaning. Built in 1856 as a navigation aid for inland waters, it is now one of the few non-coastal lighthouses in Germany—and the only one featuring a large clock on its façade.

The 33-meter-high tower was originally fueled by oil, then gas, and today its electric light serves more decorative and touristic purposes than actual maritime signaling. Nonetheless, it still marks the harbor entrance, standing proudly beside the famous Bavarian Lion statue. Together, the lighthouse and the lion form one of the most photographed harbor gateways in all of Europe.

What makes Lindau unique is its setting: freshwater waves, the backdrop of alpine mountains, and a blend of Central European architecture. Climbing the lighthouse steps—open to visitors during the summer—offers breathtaking panoramic views of Lake Constance, the rooftops of Lindau, and the Swiss and Austrian Alps beyond.

More than a maritime outpost, the Lindau Lighthouse is a living postcard, where water meets culture and German precision blends with the romantic spirit of the lake. A lighthouse that doesn't face the ocean, but reflects sunlight on freshwater—reminding us that even in the heart of continental Europe, a lantern can still tell stories of journeys, homecomings, and borders to cross.

Photo: 2012, Friedrich Böhringer/Wikimedia

Greece – Rhodes Lighthouse

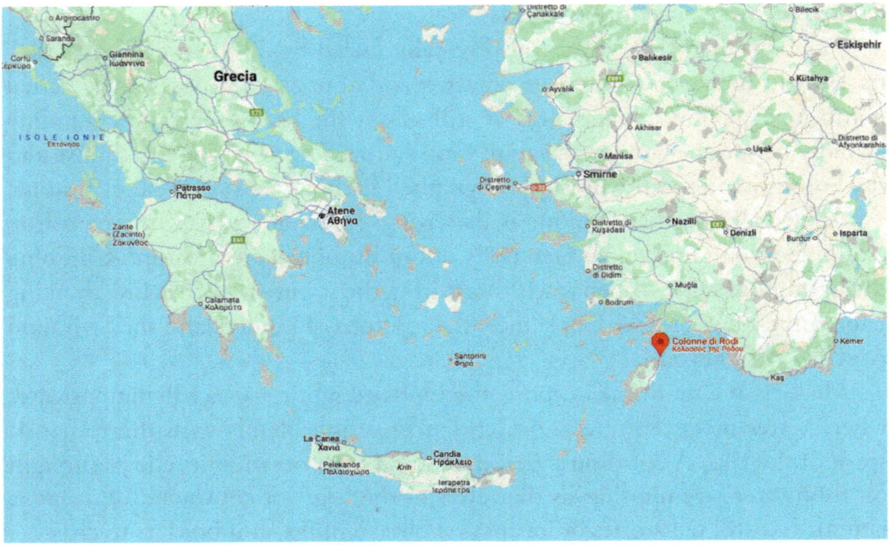

Source: Google

Lighthouse Name	Rhodes Lighthouse
Location	Port of Rhodes, Rhodes Island, Greece
Height	Unknown height – estimated between 20 and 30 m
Year Built	3rd–2nd century BCE (presumed)
Range	Estimated range: 15–20 km
Type	Stone or bronze tower – open flame on platform, possibly with mirrors
Key Features	Presumed ancient lighthouse linked to Rhodes' monumental harbor and the Colossus
Accessibility	No longer existing – no surviving structure, only archaeological hypotheses

Pl. Neoriou, Rodos 851 00, Greece	F62G+MJH Rhodes, Greece	Rhodes Lighthouse Videos and documentaries

When one thinks of ancient Rhodes, the mind immediately turns to the Colossus—the colossal bronze statue said to have stood over the harbor's entrance. Yet, less well-known but equally intriguing is the hypothesis that the same monumental port may have hosted a true lighthouse: a tower with a signal flame, possibly elevated or integrated into the city's fortifications, guiding ships into the bustling Hellenistic military and commercial harbor.

No definitive physical remains or written confirmations survive, but numerous Greek and Roman sources reference the presence of nighttime signal fires at the entrance to Rhodes' port as early as the 3rd century BCE. Some reconstructions suggest the lighthouse may have stood atop one of the two platforms at the ends of the breakwater—possibly where today stand the statues of deer, the modern symbol of the city. Unlike the towering Pharos of Alexandria, the Rhodes lighthouse likely had a more practical than symbolic purpose. It is thought to have been a stone or bronze structure, topped by an open flame lantern visible up to 15–20 kilometers under favorable conditions.

With the decline of Hellenistic rule and the natural disasters that struck the island in the centuries that followed, the supposed lighthouse vanished—along with the Colossus itself. Yet Rhodes' harbor remained a critical landmark for seafarers in the eastern Mediterranean throughout the Middle Ages.

Today, no trace remains of the original lighthouse, but the allure of the ancient harbor—where myth and history meet—still draws visitors from around the world, captivated by the idea that once, in that very spot, a guiding light shone above the waves to celebrate the island's power and welcome incoming ships.

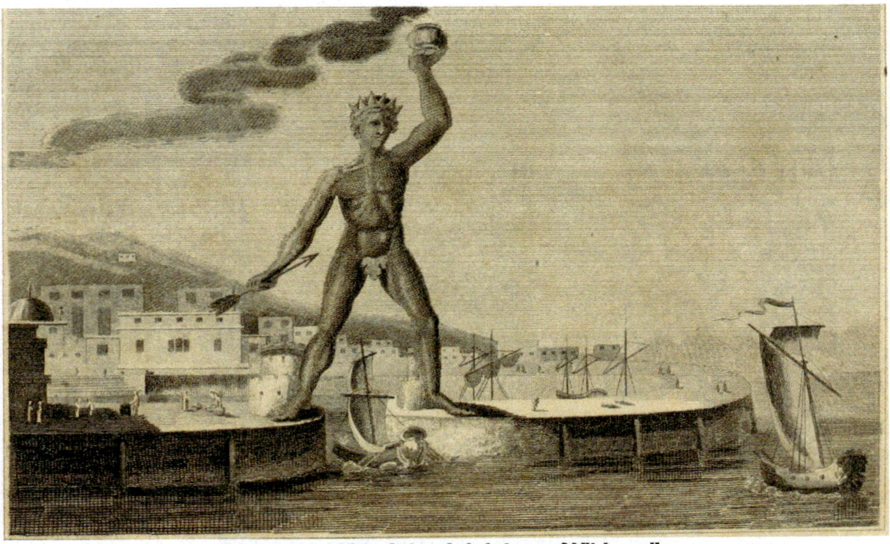

Disegno: 1821, John Adolphous/Wikimedia

Il porto di Rodi, oggi

Greece – Tourlitis Lighthouse

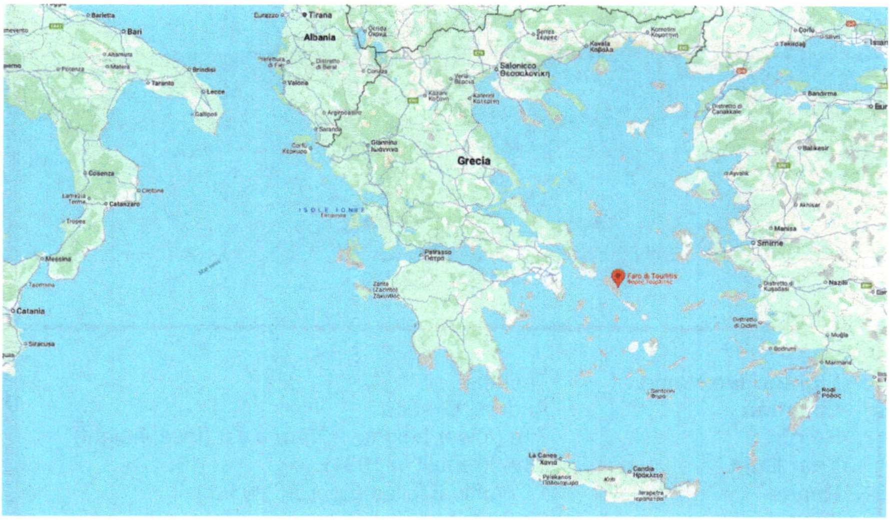

Source: Google

Source: Google

Lighthouse Name	Tourlitis
Location	Andros, Greece
Height	7 m (tower height) – 36 m a.s.l. (focal height)
Year Built	1897 (rebuilt in 1994)
Range	11 nautical miles (approx. 20 km)
Type	Stone tower on natural rock islet – solar-powered automatic light
Key Features	The only Greek lighthouse built on a natural offshore rock
Accessibility	Not accessible – visible only from the sea or Andros harbor

Andros 845 00, Greece

RWVW+6J Andro, Greece

Tourlitis Lighthouse
Videos and documentaries

More a mirage than a lighthouse, Tourlitis rises like a fairytale illustration from a jagged rock just off the port of Andros. It's one of the most unique and captivating lighthouses in the Mediterranean—Greece's only lighthouse built directly on a natural rock formation in the open sea, with no physical connection to the mainland.

Its story began in 1897, when the original structure was erected to guide ships through the treacherous approach to the island's harbor. Severely damaged during World War II, it remained inactive for decades. In 1994, however, it was faithfully reconstructed through a private initiative—a rare example of "nostalgic lighthouse restoration"—in memory of a young member of the Goulandris family, patrons of the project.

The tower itself is just 7 meters tall, but its dramatic perch makes it appear suspended between sky and sea. The light, now solar-powered and fully automated, continues to shine without human presence. Though not open to visitors, Tourlitis is clearly visible in all its splendor from the Andros waterfront or on boat trips around the island.

Tourlitis has become an emblem of Andros and one of the most photographed lighthouses in Greece. Framed by the deep blue of the Aegean and the iconic white of Cycladic architecture, it's a marvel of both engineering and poetry—an impossible lantern that still shines in the wind, telling stories more than marking routes.

Photo: 2012, Apostolispontikas/Wikimedia

Photo: 2019, Panos Vassilopoulos/Wikimedia

Iceland – Dyrhólaey Lighthouse

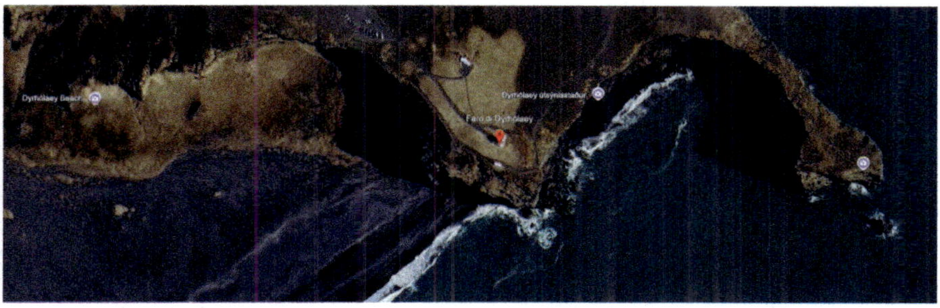

Source: Google

Photo: 2022, Pjt56/Wikimedia

Lighthouse Name	Dyrhólaey Lighthouse
Location	Vík í Mýrdal, Iceland
Height	13 m (tower height) – 118 m a.s.l. (focal height)
Year Built	1927
Range	27 nautical miles (approx. 50 km)
Type	Reinforced concrete tower in Art Deco style – automatic light
Key Features	One of the highest-positioned lighthouses above sea level in Iceland
Accessibility	Interior not accessible – scenic area freely open to visitors

CV29+VWV, 871 Vik, Iceland

CV29+VWV Dyrhólaey, 871 Vik, Iceland

Dyrhólaey Lighthouse Videos and documentaries

In southern Iceland, where cliffs plunge into the sea and the clash of fire and ice shapes otherworldly landscapes, Dyrhólaey Lighthouse stands as a silent sentinel on a headland carved by volcanoes and waves. Built in 1927 from reinforced concrete with a clean, angular silhouette that reflects Art Deco influences, it remains one of the most iconic beacons on Iceland's southern coast.

Though the tower itself is only 13 meters tall, it rises to an impressive 118 meters above sea level, perched on a black cliff overlooking the ocean and offering one of the most breathtaking views in the country. From here, visitors can admire the vast lava sand plains of Reynisfjara, the natural basalt arch formations, and even the distant Mýrdalsjökull glacier on clear days.

The light, now automated and powered by electricity, helps guide ships along this often foggy and wind-swept stretch of coast. While the interior of the lighthouse is not open to the public, the Dyrhólaey headland is freely accessible and is a prime spot for observing puffins during nesting season.

Painted white with a red roof, the lighthouse stands out as a steady point in a constantly shifting landscape—where sky, lava, and ocean converge. More than just a functional structure, it is a symbol of endurance and beauty, etched into the powerful solitude of Iceland's southern shore.

Photo: 2017, Tim Trad/Wikimedia

Ireland – Fastnet Rock Lighthouse

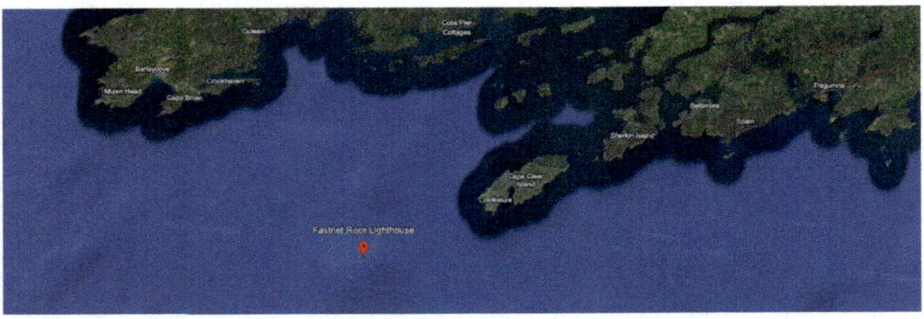

Photo: 2019, Superbass/Wikimedia

Photo: 2018, Colin Park/Wikimedia

Lighthouse Name	Fastnet Rock
Location	Off Cape Clear, County Cork, Ireland
Height	54 m (tower height) – 49 m a.s.l. (focal height)
Year Built	1904 (first lighthouse: 1854)
Range	27 nautical miles (approx. 50 km)
Type	Granite tower built with interlocking blocks – automated rotating optic
Key Features	Tallest lighthouse in Ireland – last beacon before the Atlantic for emigrant ships
Accessibility	Not accessible – visible by boat or from Cape Clear

Co. Cork, Ireland

99RV+JR Coolkelure, County Cork, Ireland

Fastnet Rock Lighthouse Videos and documentaries

Set deep in the stormy heart of the Atlantic, Fastnet Rock Lighthouse is a granite giant that has braved over a century of tempests, fog, and legend. Nicknamed "The Teardrop of Ireland," it was the last glimpse of home for millions of Irish emigrants heading to the Americas—a shining point that marked the border between hope and heartbreak. The first lighthouse, made of cast iron, was built in 1854 but soon deemed too fragile to withstand the ocean's fury. Between 1897 and 1904, the current structure was erected: a monumental tower built from interlocking granite blocks with no mortar, sourced from Scotland and individually carved to fit together like armor. Rising 54 meters above the sea, it remains the tallest lighthouse in Ireland.

The tiny islet it stands on—Fastnet Rock, also known as An Charraig Aonair ("the lonely rock")—is barely accessible, reachable only in exceptionally calm seas. For decades, teams of lighthouse keepers endured grueling shifts, cut off from the world for weeks at a time.

Automated in 1989, the lighthouse is still operational, casting its beam across 27 nautical miles. Fastnet is also famous as the namesake of one of the world's toughest offshore sailing races, the Fastnet Race, particularly remembered for the tragic 1979 edition, when a violent storm claimed the lives of 15 sailors. Today, the lighthouse is not open to visitors, but it can be admired from the sea or from the coast of Cape Clear. Even in its solitude, Fastnet stands as an epic column of stone and light—the final threshold of Europe, and the first myth of the Atlantic.

Photo: 2017, Themt Co/Wikimedia

Ireland – Fanad Head Lighthouse

Source: Google

Photo: 2008, Michal Osmenda/Wikimedia

Photo: 2012, Einaz80/Wikimedia

Lighthouse Name	Fanad Head Lighthouse
Location	Donegal, Ireland
Height	22 m (tower height) – 39 m a.s.l. (focal height)
Year Built	1817
Range	27 nautical miles (approx. 50 km)
Type	White cylindrical masonry tower – modern LED optic
Key Features	Considered one of the most scenic lighthouses in the world, part of the Wild Atlantic Way
Accessibility	Open to the public – includes tourist accommodations and visitor center

Cionn Fhánada Eara Thíre na Binne, Baile Láir, Co. Donegal, F92 YC03, Ireland

79G9+C7 Doagh Beg, County Donegal, Ireland

Fanad Head Lighthouse Videos and documentaries

At the windswept tip of the Fanad Peninsula, where the waves of the North Atlantic crash against Ireland's rugged cliffs, Fanad Head Lighthouse has stood for over two centuries as one of Europe's most picturesque and photographed beacons.

Its construction was prompted by the wreck of HMS Saldanha in 1811, a tragedy that claimed over 250 lives. When the lighthouse was first lit in 1817, it was intended to prevent such disasters from ever occurring again. Over time, the slender white tower, surrounded by windswept moors and roaring sea, became a true symbol of Ireland's Atlantic coast.

The original structure has been renovated several times and now houses a modern LED lighting system with a range of up to 27 nautical miles. But Fanad Head is more than a working lighthouse—it's a full cultural and tourism experience. Open to visitors, it offers guided tours, a visitor center, and even overnight stays in the former keepers' cottages, now transformed into elegant bed and breakfasts.

As part of the scenic Wild Atlantic Way, the lighthouse is a beacon not just for sailors but for all those seeking Ireland's wild beauty and quiet authenticity. Amid shifting skies, crashing waves, and deep silence, Fanad Head continues to cast its light across the sea—and into the hearts of all who venture to the edge.

Photo: 2014, Greg Clarke/Wikimedia

Ireland – Hook Lighthouse

Source: Google

Photo: 2023, Patrick Byrne/Wikimedia

Lighthouse Name	Hook Lighthouse
Location	Hook Head, County Wexford, Ireland
Height	35 m (tower height) – 46 m a.s.l. (focal height)
Year Built	12th century (current structure: late 1100s)
Range	23 nautical miles (approx. 43 km)
Type	Medieval stone tower with modern rotating optic
Key Features	One of the oldest operational lighthouses in the world
Accessibility	Open to the public

Hook Head, Churchtown, Co. Wexford, Ireland

43FC+F7 Churchtown, County Wexford, Ireland

Hook Lighthouse Videos and documentaries

At the tip of the Hook Peninsula in County Wexford stands Hook Lighthouse—believed to be the oldest lighthouse in the world still in operation. Its massive limestone tower dates back more than 800 years, built around the year 1200, possibly by the Welsh monk Saint Dubhán or, according to other sources, by Norman knights to guard the maritime approach to Waterford Harbor.

The original beacon was a wood-burning fire lit atop the tower, later replaced by oil lamps and eventually by a fully automated modern light system. The 35-meter-high tower still retains many of its medieval features, including stone spiral staircases, vaulted ceilings, and narrow slit windows. It is a marvel of functional architecture, having withstood the test of time, storms, and even war.

Today, the lighthouse remains operational and is also a popular heritage site. It houses a visitor center with exhibits, a café, and guided tours that take guests all the way to the top. Each step retraces centuries of history—from monastic origins to the age of keepers and its current role as a cultural landmark.

From the headland, sweeping views open across the Celtic Sea, with steady winds and, on clear days, sightings of seals, dolphins, and even whales. But the real magic lies in the union of stone and light, where the past endures not in silence but with renewed brilliance—an ancient monument that continues to shine.

Photo: 2015, Andrew Sykes/Wikimedia

Italy – Lanterna di Genova

Source: Google

A timeless symbol of one of Italy's greatest maritime cities, the Lanterna di Genova is more than a lighthouse—it is identity, history, and architecture rising from the harbor like a sentinel between land and sea. Standing 77 meters tall and reaching a focal height of 117 meters above sea level, it is the tallest historic lighthouse in the Mediterranean and the second highest in Europe after Île Vierge in Brittany.

The current structure dates back to 1543, but the original tower was built in 1128, with a flame fueled first by wood, then oil. Over the centuries, the Lanterna has witnessed Genoa's fortunes and storms: seen from afar by merchants, feared by pirates, bombed and rebuilt. Today it remains one of the oldest operational lighthouses in the world and serves as an emblem on the city's coat of arms.

Built from stone, the lighthouse is composed of two stacked square sections and topped by a modern automated lantern that emits a beam visible up to 25 nautical miles, still marking the entrance to Genoa's busy port. At its base lies the Lanterna Museum, which tells the story of the lighthouse and the city through historical documents, models, and optical instruments.

The Lanterna is open to visitors. A raised walkway connects it to the center of Genoa, winding through a once-industrial zone now transformed into a cultural space. From the top, visitors enjoy a breathtaking view over the Ligurian Gulf, with its blend of cargo terminals, coastal cliffs, and shimmering seas. Its light does more than guide ships—it keeps alive the memory of a city whose very soul is tied to the sea. This is not just any lighthouse: this is the Lanterna.

Lighthouse Name	Lanterna di Genova
Location	Genoa, Italy
Height	77 m (tower height) – 117 m above sea level (focal height)
Year Built	1543 (original base from 1128)
Range	25 nautical miles (approx. 46 km)
Type	Masonry tower with two stacked square sections – rotating automatic light
Key Features	Tallest historic lighthouse in the Mediterranean – symbol of Genoa
Accessibility	Open to the public

Lanterna di Genova,
Piazzale S. Benigno, 16149
Genova GE, Italy

CW33+RV Genova, Italy

Lanterna di Genova
Videos and documentaries

Photo: 2014, Daniele Tassiano/Wikimedia

Italy – Punta Carena Lighthouse

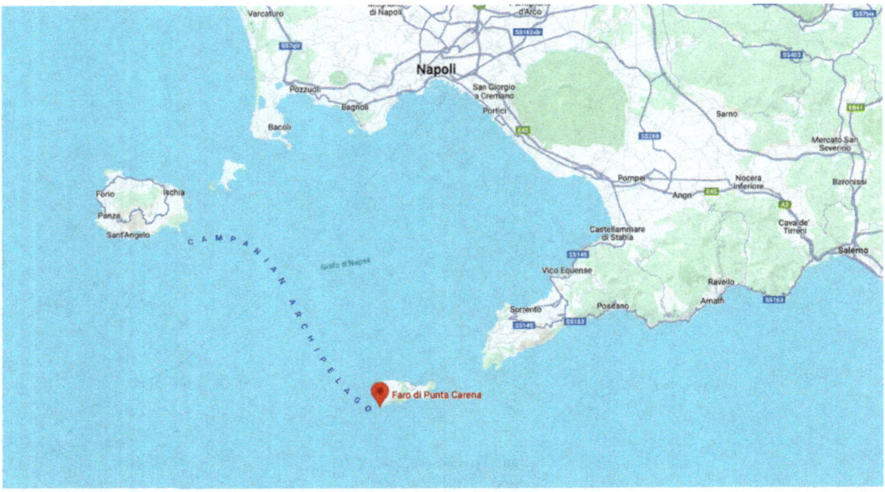

Source: Google

Lighthouse Name	Punta Carena Lighthouse
Location	Anacapri, Italy
Height	28 m (tower height)
Year Built	1866–1867
Range	25 nautical miles (approx. 46 km)
Type	Octagonal masonry tower with white lantern on red base
Key Features	Active, automated lighthouse – second tallest in Italy after the Genoa Lantern
Accessibility	Not open to the public (interior)

Via Faro Punta Carena,
80071 Anacapri NA, Italy

40°32'12"N 14°11'50"E

Punta Carena Lighthouse
Videos and documentaries

Nestled among the rocky cliffs at the southwestern tip of Capri, the Punta Carena Lighthouse is a striking blend of architectural elegance and maritime resilience. For over 150 years, it has watched over the waters of the Tyrrhenian Sea with unwavering presence. Built between 1866 and 1867, it is the second tallest lighthouse in Italy, after Genoa's famed Lanterna, and remained one of the few still inhabited by lighthouse keepers until recent times.

Its octagonal masonry tower, painted in distinctive red and white stripes, stands atop a wind-battered promontory, offering panoramic views of the gulf and the imaginary line connecting Mount Vesuvius to the Pontine Islands. The beam reaches nearly 46 kilometers across the sea, guiding maritime traffic entering and leaving Naples and the Procida Channel. Though now fully automated, the lighthouse has preserved its primary function. While the interior is not open to visitors, the surrounding area is accessible and beloved by both locals and tourists. The rocky shoreline serves as a tranquil sunbathing spot, prized for its silence and rugged beauty—especially at sunset.

Over time, the Punta Carena Lighthouse has also become a romantic symbol of the island, featured in postcards, paintings, and films, all while maintaining its austere calling as a sentinel of the sea.

Photo: 2016, Nemo/Wikimedia

Photo: 2007, Hardo Müller/Wikimedia

Italy – Punta Penna Lighthouse

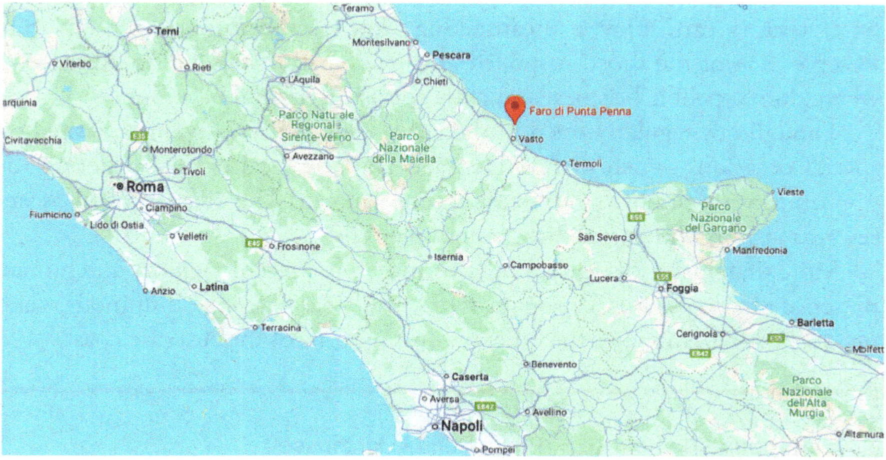

Perched on a rocky promontory overlooking the Adriatic, the Punta Penna Lighthouse rises with a commanding presence along the Abruzzo coastline. At 70 meters tall, it is the second tallest lighthouse in Italy—after the Lanterna of Genoa—and one of the tallest in all of Europe. Its slender white silhouette is visible from miles away, a reassuring beacon for sailors and a reference point for the entire central Adriatic coast.

The original lighthouse was lit in 1906 but was destroyed during World War II. The current structure was rebuilt in 1948 using reinforced concrete, resulting in a solid, functional octagonal tower. Fully automated today, its lantern projects light up to 25 nautical miles, guiding vessels along one of the Adriatic's busiest routes, between the ports of Ortona and Termoli.

Despite its primarily technical purpose, the lighthouse holds deep emotional value for the town of Vasto and the surrounding region. From its base, visitors can enjoy a breathtaking view of the Punta Aderci Nature Reserve, one of the most unspoiled and wild coastal stretches in Abruzzo—where dunes, pebble beaches, and cliffs coexist in natural harmony.

Though not regularly open to the public, the lighthouse can be visited on special occasions—such as FAI Heritage Days or local events—offering the opportunity to climb its 307 steps to the lantern. The steep vertical ascent rewards visitors with a stunning panoramic view.

More than just a structure, Punta Penna is a bastion of memory and human presence in constant dialogue with the sea. Strong, luminous, and unadorned—it embodies the quiet, enduring spirit of the Adriatic coast.

Lighthouse Name	Punta Penna Lighthouse
Location	Vasto, Abruzzo, Italy
Height	70 m (tower height) – 92 m a.s.l. (focal height)
Year Built	1906 (rebuilt in 1948)
Range	25 nautical miles (approx. 46 km)
Type	Octagonal reinforced concrete tower – automated rotating light
Key Features	Second tallest lighthouse in Italy – key reference point for the central Adriatic
Accessibility	Open to the public on special occasions

Via Punta Penna, 66054 Zona Industriale Porto di Vasto CH, Italy

42°10′12″N 14°42′54″E

Punta Penna Lighthouse Videos and documentaries

Photo: 2010, Zitumassin/Wikimedia

Italy – Ravenna Lighthouse

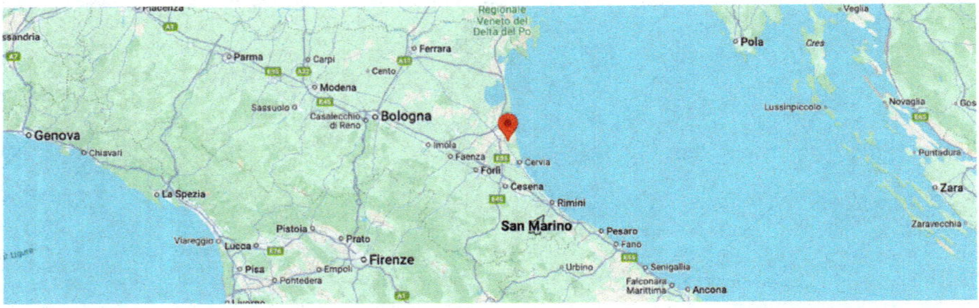

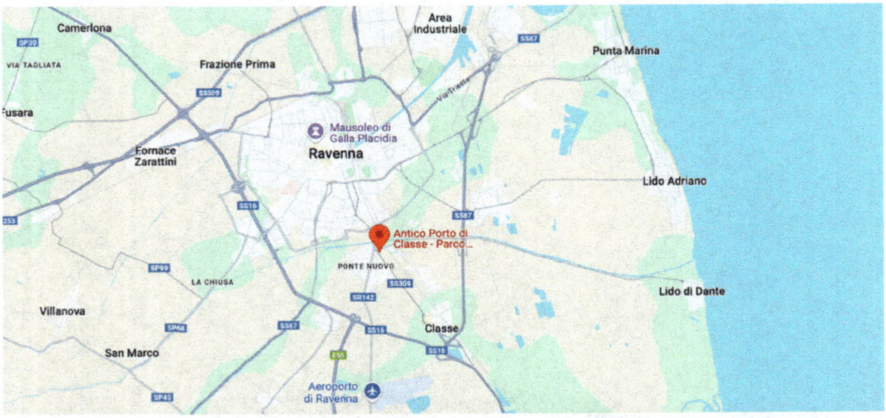

Source: Google

Lighthouse Name	Ravenna Lighthouse
Location	Classe, Ravenna, Italy
Height	Estimated height: 20–25 m
Year Built	Imperial Roman era – 1st or 2nd century CE
Range	Range unknown – open flame and daytime visual signals
Type	Masonry structure, likely a cylindrical tower on a square base
Key Features	Port and military function – lighthouse of the Imperial Roman fleet
Accessibility	No longer exists – no visible remains; presumed location near the ancient port of Classe

Via Marabina, 7 Zona Ponte Nuovo-Classe, 48124 Ravenna RA, Italy	96W8+7V Ravenna, Italy	Ravenna Lighthouse Videos and documentaries

In the 1st century CE, Ravenna became the headquarters of the Classis Praetoria Ravennatis, the powerful naval fleet of the Western Roman Empire. To support this massive military presence, the port of Classe was constructed—one of the most active harbors of antiquity. Along with it, according to several sources, a coastal lighthouse was also built, though it has not survived to the present day.

While no visible remains exist, written records and archaeological evidence support the likely presence of a lighthouse tower, estimated to have stood between 20 and 25 meters tall. Built in masonry, the structure likely featured a cylindrical shaft atop a square base—consistent with similar Roman-era buildings. Its purpose was both civil and strategic: guiding the Imperial fleet, marking the entrance to the navigable canal connecting Ravenna to the sea, and coordinating the movements of warships and cargo vessels.

The lighthouse is thought to have remained in use at least until the 6th century, when sediment began to accumulate, gradually burying the harbor. Over the centuries, the entire port disappeared. Today, the memory of the lighthouse survives only in historical texts and symbolic depictions—most notably in the mosaic of Sant'Apollinare in Classe, located just steps from where the structure likely once stood.

The Ravenna lighthouse represents a vital link between the Hellenistic-Roman tradition and the medieval evolution of coastal beacons. It may not have been as monumental as the Pharos of Alexandria, or as legendary as the lighthouse of Rhodes, but it was undeniably functional—an essential element of one of the Roman Mediterranean's strategic maritime hubs.

Ancient port of Classe – Photo: Ravenna Antica

Italy – Strombolicchio Lighthouse

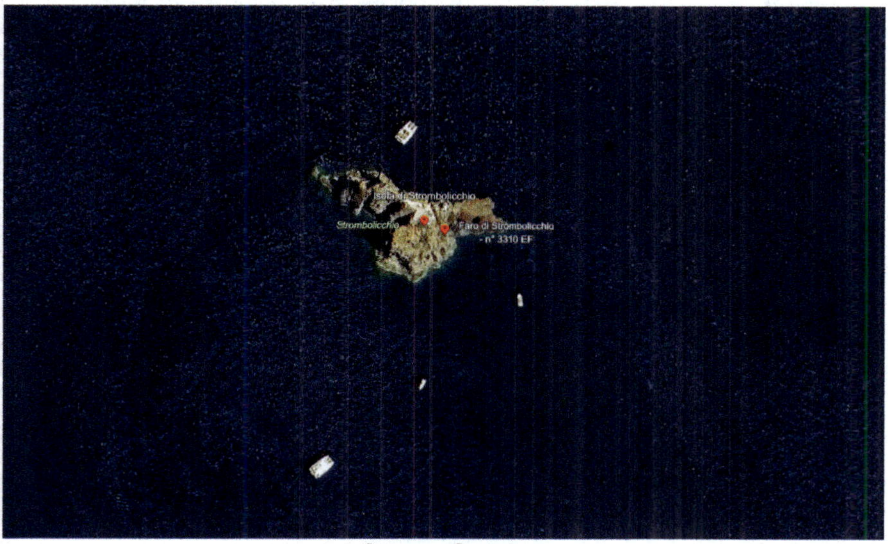

Source: Google

Photo: 2007, Giovanni/Wikimedia

Lighthouse Name	Strombolicchio Lighthouse
Location	Stromboli, Aeolian Islands, Sicily, Italy
Height	8 m (tower height) – 57 m above sea level (focal height)
Year Built	1925
Range	11 nautical miles (approx. 20 km)
Type	Cylindrical concrete tower on volcanic islet – solar-powered automatic light
Key Features	Solitary lighthouse atop a volcanic neck – unique view over the archipelago
Accessibility	Not accessible – visible only from the sea

Faro di Strombolicchio - n° 3310 E.F, 98050 Stromboli ME, Italy

R782+WR Stromboli, Messina, Italy

Strombolicchio Lighthouse Videos and documentaries

Atop a dramatic tower of black lava—born from a prehistoric eruption—stands one of the most isolated and iconic lighthouses in the Mediterranean: Strombolicchio Lighthouse, a silent sentinel off the coast of Stromboli. We're in the Aeolian Islands, an archipelago of fire and wind, where nature speaks a primordial language and humans can only adapt.

Strombolicchio is the eroded remnant of an ancient volcanic cone—a basalt neck carved over centuries by wind and sea. Perched on its summit is a small cylindrical concrete tower, built in 1925 and visible from all over the island. The lighthouse, now fully automated and powered by solar energy, emits a beam reaching up to 11 nautical miles.

A staircase carved directly into the rock leads to the top, but access is restricted for safety and environmental reasons. From land, the profile of Strombolicchio—with the lighthouse like a white "cap" crowning the dark rock—resembles both a natural sculpture and an architectural marvel, a perfect harmony of geology and engineering.

This lighthouse is more than a navigational aid: it's a symbol of solitude and endurance. It marks the far edge from which one can gaze back toward Stromboli, watching the volcano erupt night after night. Despite its modest size, it's among the most photographed and beloved lighthouses by travelers seeking silence and raw beauty.

It is a lighthouse on a mountain in the sea—and no description could be more poetic.

Italy – Victory Lighthouse

Photo: 2008, Tiesse/Wikimedia

Lighthouse Name	Faro della Vittoria (Victory Lighthouse)
Location	Trieste, Friuli Venezia Giulia, Italy
Height	68.85 m (tower height) – 115 m a.s.l. (focal height)
Year Built	1927
Range	22 nautical miles (approx. 41 km)
Type	Monumental tower made of karst stone and reinforced concrete – automatic light
Key Features	Memorial lighthouse honoring sailors fallen in World War I
Accessibility	Open to the public – panoramic viewpoint accessible during specific hours

Str. del Friuli, 141, 34136
Trieste TS, Italy

MQG4+7Q Trieste, Italy

Victory Lighthouse
Videos and documentaries

Imposing, solemn, and visible from every corner of the Gulf of Trieste, the Faro della Vittoria is more than just a navigational aid—it is a national monument that blends maritime function with historical memory. Inaugurated in 1927, it was conceived to honor the sailors who perished in World War I and has since become one of the city's most iconic landmarks.

Designed by architect Arduino Berlam, the lighthouse was built using local karst stone and reinforced concrete. It rises nearly 69 meters, with its strategic placement on Gretta Hill elevating its focal height to 115 meters above sea level. At its summit stands a bronze statue of Winged Victory, while at its base lies the anchor of the destroyer Audace, the first Italian ship to enter the port of Trieste in 1918.

The light, now fully automated, reaches 22 nautical miles and guides ships approaching the port of Trieste. But what makes this lighthouse truly unique among European beacons is its dual identity—both technical and commemorative. Every element, from the lantern to the sculptural symbolism, evokes a transitional era marked by war, national reunification, and the enduring link between sea and homeland.

The lighthouse is open to visitors at certain times of the year, allowing access to a mid-level observation deck with breathtaking views of the city, the karst plateau, and the Adriatic Sea. At sunset, the light filtering through the marble columns and sculpted reliefs conveys the sense of a place that guides not only ships—but also collective memory. It is not merely a lighthouse: it is the Lantern of Trieste's history.

Photo: 2019, Andrzej Otrębski/Wikimedia

Photo: 2007, Guido Radig/Wikimedia

Photo: 2008, Tiesse/Wikimedia

Japan – Enoshima Sea Candle

Source: Google

Photo: Japan Travel Magazine

Lighthouse Name	Enoshima Lighthouse (Enoshima Sea Candle)
Location	Fujisawa, Kanagawa Prefecture, Japan
Height	59.8 m (structure height) – 101.5 m a.s.l. (focal height)
Year Built	2003 (original tower: 1951)
Range	N/A (observation tower with decorative lighting)
Type	Steel and glass observation tower – LED lighting
Key Features	Urban and touristic lighthouse – architectural symbol of Sagami Bay
Accessibility	Open to the public

2 Chome-3-28 Enoshima, Fujisawa, Kanagawa 251-0036, Japan

7FXH+V9 Fujisawa, Kanagawa, Japan

Enoshima Sea Candle Videos and documentaries

More than a traditional lighthouse, the Enoshima Lighthouse—also known as the Enoshima Sea Candle—is an elegant observation tower that blends decorative function, contemporary architecture, and touristic appeal. Located on the small island of Enoshima, connected to the mainland by a pedestrian bridge, it is one of the most beloved landmarks overlooking Sagami Bay, just south of Tokyo. The original tower was erected in 1951, but the current structure—nearly 60 meters tall and situated on a hill that raises its focal height to over 100 meters above sea level—was completed in 2003 to commemorate the 100th anniversary of the Port of Yokohama. Made of steel and glass with an airy, modern design, the Sea Candle is visible for kilometers both day and night, thanks to its multicolored LED illumination.

Though not a functioning maritime lighthouse in the traditional sense, the tower serves as an iconic visual landmark for both seafarers along the coast and tourists visiting the island. Open year-round, it features both an elevator and a staircase leading to an open-air observation deck that offers 360-degree views—on clear days, one can see Mount Fuji, Tokyo, the Pacific coast, and even the Japanese Alps.

Surrounded by the scenic Samuel Cocking Garden, the Sea Candle is part of a landscape that combines nature, history, and contemporary design. By night, it becomes an urban lantern—a romantic and cultural beacon for the entire Shōnan region. It is a 21st-century lighthouse: not just to illuminate the sea, but to celebrate the landscape and the life that surrounds it.

Photo: GaijinPot

Japan – Inubōsaki Lighthouse

Source: Google

Lighthouse Name	Inubōsaki Lighthouse
Location	Chōshi, Chiba Prefecture, Japan
Height	31 m (tower height) – 52 m a.s.l. (focal height)
Year Built	1874
Range	19 nautical miles (approx. 35 km)
Type	White brick cylindrical tower – first-order Fresnel lens
Key Features	One of the first modern Japanese lighthouses – built by British engineer
Accessibility	Open to the public – lantern access and adjacent museum

9576 Inubosaki, Choshi, Chiba 288-0012, Japan

PV59+5C Chōshi, Chiba, Japan

Inubōsaki Lighthouse Videos and documentaries

At the easternmost tip of Japan's main island of Honshū, where the sun rises first over the nation, the Inubōsaki Lighthouse stands proudly above the Pacific Ocean, combining elegant form with deep historical roots. Built in 1874, it is one of the earliest lighthouses of the Meiji era, designed by renowned British engineer Richard Henry Brunton, who played a key role in modernizing Japan's maritime infrastructure after the end of the feudal period.

The 31-meter-tall white brick tower houses a spiral staircase leading up to a still-operational first-order Fresnel lens—one of the largest and most powerful of its kind. Its beam guides vessels approaching the Chōshi coast, a region prone to strong currents and sudden fog. With a range of 19 nautical miles, the lighthouse continues to operate using modern technology, while preserving its original structure and spirit.

But Inubōsaki is more than just a functional beacon—it is also a cultural and touristic destination. Open to visitors, the lighthouse allows access to the lantern room, offering breathtaking views of the ocean and rugged coastline. Nearby, a small museum tells the story of Japan's lighthouse system and 19th-century maritime engineering.

In every season, the Inubōsaki headland attracts tourists and photographers eager to witness the sunrise—the symbolic moment when Japan awakens. For this reason, the lighthouse has also become a symbol of renewal and guidance, a steadfast presence in a changing world, like the light that has sliced through the darkness each morning for a century and a half.

Photo: 2013, Takashi Hososhima/Wikimedia

Libya – Leptis Magna Lighthouse

Source: Google

Lighthouse Name	Leptis Magna Lighthouse
Location	Leptis Magna, near Al Khums, Libya
Height	Estimated height: over 35 m
Year Built	Roman era – late 1st century AD
Range	Unknown range – likely between 20 and 30 km
Type	Monumental square-plan tower on stepped base
Key Features	Part of a monumental harbor complex – among the most advanced in the Roman world
Accessibility	Completely disappeared – only base remnants remain

J8R2+3JC, Leptis Magna, Libya

J8R2+3JC

Leptis Magna Lighthouse Videos and documentaries

At the southern edge of the Mediterranean, within the breathtaking archaeological site of Leptis Magna—a once-flourishing Roman port in Tripolitania—stood one of the most remarkable lighthouses of antiquity. Likely built in the late 1st century AD, this monumental structure rose more than 35 meters above the African coastline and was visible for miles out at sea.

Historical sources and archaeological studies describe a massive square-plan tower built on a stepped platform, echoing the design of the famous Pharos of Alexandria with which it shared several engineering traits. Not coincidentally, the Leptis Magna lighthouse is considered one of the finest examples of Roman maritime architecture, combining practical function, monumental scale, and symbolic visibility. Located at the entrance to the city's eastern harbor, facing the open sea, the lighthouse guided both merchant and military vessels along key trade routes connecting Carthage, Rome, and Alexandria—making it a strategic hub in the imperial Mediterranean. Ancient iconography and reliefs depict a multi-tiered tower with a lantern at the top and a spiral staircase within, similar to other Roman lighthouses of the time.

Today, only the squared stone foundation remains, gazing out over the sea. Yet the lighthouse's role in maritime history and Roman engineering is widely acknowledged. Leptis Magna itself—now a UNESCO World Heritage Site—still boasts extraordinary ruins of temples, forums, and harbor works. Amidst them, the lost lighthouse lives on as a radiant symbol of Rome's maritime power.

Photo: 2011, Roger Pearse

New Zeland – Cape Reinga Lighthouse

Source: Google

Photo: 2010, Or Hiltch/Wikimedia

Lighthouse Name	Cape Reinga Lighthouse
Location	Cape Reinga, Northland, New Zealand
Height	10 m (tower height) – 165 m a.s.l. (focal height)
Year Built	1941 (relocated from Cape Maria van Diemen)
Range	19 nautical miles (approx. 35 km)
Type	Cylindrical steel tower – automated light powered by solar energy
Key Features	Symbolic lighthouse at the northern tip of New Zealand – sacred site in Māori culture
Accessibility	Not accessible inside – scenic site open to visitors

Cape Reinga 0484, New Zeland

HMFH+72 Cape Reinga, New Zeland

Cape Reinga Lighthouse Videos and documentaries

At the northernmost tip of New Zealand, where the Tasman Sea meets the Pacific Ocean, stands the Cape Reinga Lighthouse—small in size but immense in meaning. It is the country's most famous lighthouse, not so much for its maritime function as for its symbolic position and deep spiritual connection to Māori culture.

Built in 1941 and now powered by solar energy, the lighthouse is fully automated and projects its beam up to 19 nautical miles. The tower itself is only 10 meters tall, but it sits atop a steep headland 165 meters above sea level, offering one of the most dramatic and awe-inspiring views in the Southern Hemisphere.

According to Māori tradition, Cape Reinga—Te Rerenga Wairua, "the leaping place of spirits"—is where the souls of the dead depart the land of the living and begin their journey to the afterlife. At the base of the cliff, an ancient pōhutukawa tree juts out over the rocks. Legend says that from this tree, spirits dive into the ocean on their way back to Hawaiki, the ancestral homeland.

Though the lighthouse itself is not open to visitors, the surrounding site is fully accessible via a serene, landscaped walking path. Next to the tower stands the famous signpost showing distances to world capitals—a photo op and iconic image of New Zealand.

Cape Reinga is more than a tourist destination: it is a physical and spiritual threshold where light, oceans, and culture converge. A lighthouse that doesn't just guide ships, but also the reflections of all who gaze out from the edge of the world.

Photo: 2019, Uliana Ilchenko/Wikimedia

Norway – Kjeungskjær Lighthouse

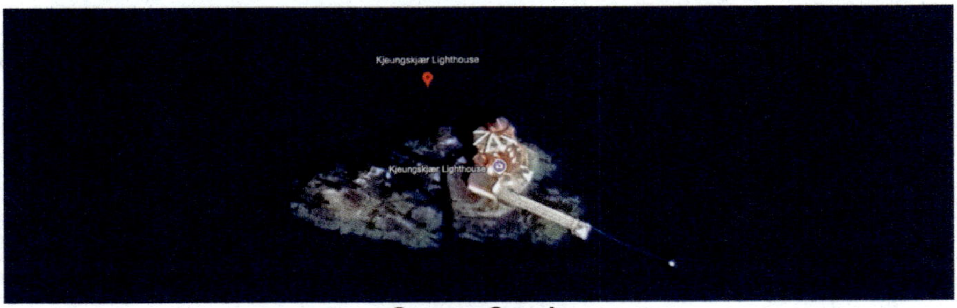

Source: Google

Photo: 2016, Gordon Leggett/Wikimedia

Photo: 2023, Sivbenteu/Wikimedia

Lighthouse Name	Kjeungskjær Lighthouse
Location	Ørland, Trøndelag, Norway
Height	20.6 m
Year Built	1880
Range	13 nautical miles (approx. 24 km)
Type	Octagonal red brick tower on islet – automated light
Key Features	One of Norway's most picturesque lighthouses – residential lighthouse on isolated islet
Accessibility	Not accessible – visible only by boat or from a distance

Postboks 3, 7129 Brekstad, Norway

PGGJ+P7 Uthaug, Norway

Kjeungskjær Lighthouse Videos and documentaries

In the heart of Norway's fjords, where the Norwegian Sea weaves between islands and rocky outcrops, stands a lighthouse that looks like it came straight out of a Nordic watercolor painting: Kjeungskjær Lighthouse. Built in 1880 at the entrance to the Bjugn Fjord in the Trøndelag region, this 20.6-meter octagonal red brick tower rises from a tiny rocky islet, alone in the sea, its white-trimmed windows and pointed roof lending it a storybook charm.

What sets Kjeungskjær apart is not its height, but the harmony of its colors and its unique setting. It's one of the few residential lighthouses ever built on such remote islets. Until it was fully automated in 1987, it housed entire families of lighthouse keepers—often with young children—who led lives of solitude, courage, and daily rituals surrounded by waves and weather.

Its beacon, now automated, shines up to 13 nautical miles and continues to serve as a navigational aid while the structure itself is protected as a national cultural heritage site. Over the years, Kjeungskjær has become famous for its fairy-tale appearance and is now one of the most photographed lighthouses in Norway. From land, it can be spotted only through long-range lenses, while boat tours in summer sometimes offer closer views—though landing on the islet is prohibited for safety and preservation reasons.

Kjeungskjær doesn't just guide ships—it stirs the imagination. With its timeless elegance and enchanted solitude, it stands as a poetic sentinel in the Scandinavian seascape.

Photo: 2023, Wolfgang Fricke/Wikimedia

Portugal – Cabo da Roca Lighthouse

Source: Google

Photo: 2012, CEphoto, Uwe Aranas/Wikimedia

Lighthouse Name	Cabo da Roca Lighthouse
Location	Cascais, Lisbon District, Portugal
Height	22 m (tower height) – 165 m a.s.l. (focal height)
Year Built	1772
Range	26 nautical miles (approx. 48 km)
Type	Square masonry tower with red lantern – automated light
Key Features	Westernmost lighthouse of mainland Europe – built atop a high ocean cliff
Accessibility	Not accessible inside – panoramic site open to visitors

Colares, Portugal

QGJ3+Q3 Colares, Portugal

Cabo da Roca Lighthouse Videos and documentaries

At the westernmost point of mainland Europe, where land ends and the sea begins, rises the Cabo da Roca Lighthouse—ancient sentinel of the Atlantic Ocean. Perched on a towering cliff 165 meters above sea level, the lighthouse has watched over the Portuguese coastline for more than two and a half centuries.

Built in 1772, it is one of the oldest lighthouses in Portugal still in operation. The 22-meter tower, topped by a red lantern, stands above a traditional masonry service building, characteristic of 18th-century Portuguese coastal architecture. Its light, now fully automated, reaches up to 26 nautical miles and continues to guide vessels navigating the northeastern Atlantic routes.

But Cabo da Roca is more than just a beacon—it is a symbolic and literary landmark, immortalized by Portuguese poet Luís de Camões as "the place where the land ends and the sea begins" (Onde a terra se acaba e o mar começa). Today, the lighthouse watches over a majestic landscape swept by wind and lined with cliffside trails and vertical bluffs, attracting travelers and photographers from around the world.

The site is freely accessible, although the lighthouse itself is closed to the public. A stone plaque and a commemorative cross greet visitors, marking the extreme and poetic nature of the promontory's location. At sunset, the lantern's light flickers on as the sky turns golden and the ocean roars beneath the cliffs.

Cabo da Roca is both boundary and horizon, rock and light—a lighthouse marking Europe's final step into the unknown.

Photo: 2019, Sonse/Wikimedia

Russia – Tolbukhin Lighthouse

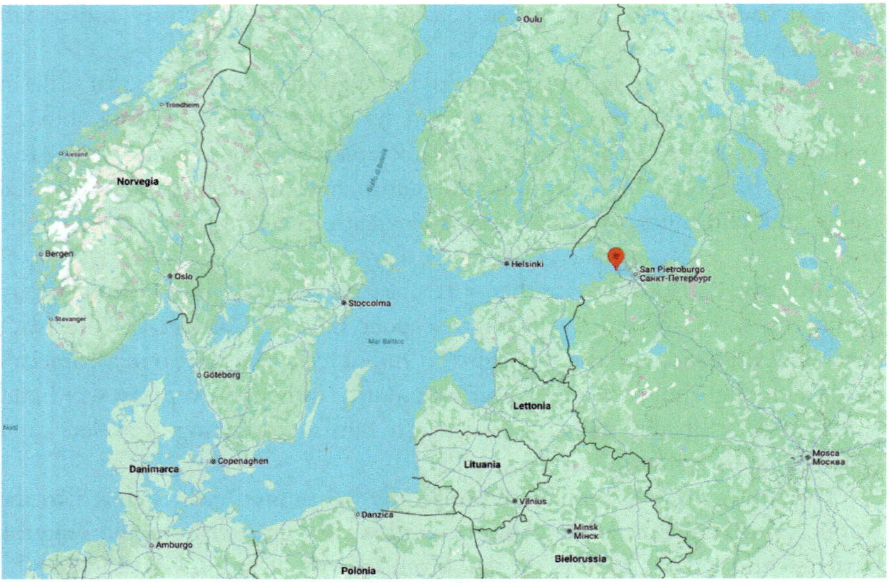

Source: Google

Photo: 2012, gordey2003/Wikimedia

Photo: 2011, APVla/Wikimedia

Lighthouse Name	Tolbukhin
Location	Gulf of Finland, Saint Petersburg, Russia
Height	32 m (tower height) – 38 m a.s.l. (focal height)
Year Built	1719 (rebuilt 1810–1816)
Range	18 nautical miles (approx. 33 km)
Type	Cylindrical stone and masonry tower – automatic light
Key Features	Oldest lighthouse on the Russian Baltic coast – commissioned by Peter the Great
Accessibility	Not accessible – visible only by sea

60°02'33.0"N 29°32'31.0"E

60°02'33.0"N 29°32'31.0"E

Tolbukhin Lighthouse
Videos and documentaries

Off the coast of Saint Petersburg, in the frigid waters of the Gulf of Finland, stands the Tolbukhin Lighthouse—the oldest lighthouse on the Russian side of the Baltic Sea. Commissioned in 1719 by Peter the Great himself, it was built to safeguard maritime access to his newly founded imperial capital. The lighthouse rises from a tiny artificial islet, solitary and windswept, often encircled by ice and battered by Baltic storms.

The current white stone and masonry tower was reconstructed between 1810 and 1816, after the original wooden structure was destroyed. Standing 32 meters tall, its light now reaches up to 18 nautical miles and is fully automated.

Its position is as strategic as it is remote: not open to the public, and surprisingly hard to locate—even with modern digital tools. A search on Google Maps might yield nothing: the islet is not marked as a tourist site and is nearly invisible, lacking any official place name or label. Only with precise coordinates (60°02′33″ N, 29°32′31″ E) or advanced mapping platforms like OpenStreetMap or Mapcarta can one pinpoint its true location. This makes it a lighthouse quite literally off the map.

Renamed in Soviet times in honor of General Fyodor Tolbukhin, the lighthouse has endured centuries of war, ice, and isolation. During the Siege of Leningrad, it served as both a symbolic and navigational beacon for naval and civilian resistance. Today, its silent light still tells stories of empires, endurance, and solitude—largely unseen, but ever present amid the mists and waters of the Baltic Sea.

Photo: 2011, APVla/Wikimedia

Spain – Hercules Tower

Source: Google

Photo: 2015, Diego Delso/Wikimedia

Lighthouse Name	Torre de Hércules (Hercules Tower)
Location	La Coruña, Galicia, Spain
Height	55 m (total height including modern base)
Year Built	2nd century AD (renovated in the 18th century)
Range	24 nautical miles (approx. 44 km)
Type	Roman square-base structure with neoclassical restoration – automated electric light
Key Features	Oldest lighthouse in the world still in operation – UNESCO World Heritage Site
Accessibility	Open to the public – interior accessible to visitors

Av. Navarra, s/n, 15002 A Coruña, Spain

9HPV+9C La Coruña, Spain

Hercules Tower
Videos and documentaries

Perched on a wind-swept promontory overlooking the Atlantic Ocean, in the Galician city of La Coruña, stands a lighthouse that has spanned nearly two thousand years of history: the Tower of Hercules. It is considered the oldest Roman lighthouse still in operation in the world—and the only one to survive intact and functional, though significantly modified.

Built between the 1st and 2nd centuries AD by engineers of the Roman Empire, it was designed to guide navigation along the northwestern coast of Hispania, a strategic location for maritime trade routes to the British Isles. Originally about 34 meters high and built on a square plan, it featured a platform at the top where fires were lit to signal passing ships.

Over the centuries, the tower fell into disuse and was partially buried under debris and sand until, in the 18th century, it was restored and raised in height in a neoclassical style by architect Eustaquio Giannini, under commission from the Spanish Crown. Today it stands at 55 meters and houses an automated lighting system.

The Tower of Hercules has become a powerful symbol of Galician identity, earning its place as a UNESCO World Heritage Site in 2009. Open to the public, it offers breathtaking views of the ocean and contains a preserved Roman stone staircase within. More than a lighthouse, it is a bridge between civilizations—a monument uniting ancient Roman ingenuity with modern maritime technology. Its light, still shining today, does not merely illuminate the sea—it tells a story of resilience, knowledge, and beauty stretching across the centuries.

2011, Bugallo Sánchez/Wikimedia

2008, F.L. Rodríguez/Wikimedia

Sweden – Pater Noster Lighthouse

Source: Google

Photo: 2015, HasBS/Wikimedia

Lighthouse Name	Pater Noster Lighthouse
Location	Hamneskär Island, Västra Götaland, Sweden
Height	32 m
Year Built	1868
Range	21 nautical miles (approx. 39 km)
Type	Red cast-iron octagonal lattice tower
Key Features	Historic lighthouse on wind-swept rock – now an exclusive hotel
Accessibility	No longer active as a lighthouse – accessible by reservation (private lodging)

471 51 Arvidsvik, Sweden

VFW8+C9 Arvidsvik, Sweden

Pater Noster Lighthouse Videos and documentaries

Off the rugged western coast of Sweden, on a barren rock lashed by the winds of the northern Atlantic, stands Pater Noster—one of Scandinavia's most striking and photographed lighthouses. Its name, Latin for "Our Father," echoes the prayer once murmured by sailors before braving the treacherous waters between the Marstrand archipelago and Hamneskär Island.

Built in 1868 and designed by Gustaf von Heidenstam, the lighthouse is a slender red iron structure with an octagonal open-frame design—one of the first of its kind in Europe. Standing 32 meters tall, its beam once reached 21 nautical miles, guiding ships through the fog and rocks of the Kattegat for more than a century. The light was finally extinguished in 2007, marking the end of its service as a navigational aid.

Yet the story of Pater Noster did not end there. Thanks to a carefully executed architectural restoration, it has found new life as a one-of-a-kind boutique hotel. Accessible only by sea and with reservation, the site now offers elite accommodations within the refurbished keepers' quarters—blending Nordic wilderness with minimalist luxury. Visitors can walk across the rocky islet, hear the wind hum through the tower's iron braces, and gaze out toward the endless horizon.

Pater Noster is more than a decommissioned lighthouse—it's a prayer suspended between sea and sky, reborn as a sanctuary for those seeking beauty, silence, and solitude at the edge of the world.

Photo: 2015, HasBS/Wikimedia

Turkey – Maiden's Tower

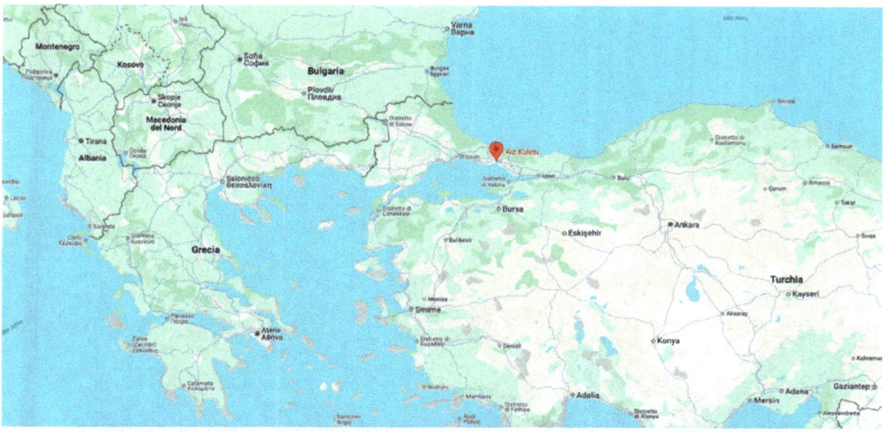

Source: Google

Photo: 2021, Sonse/Wikimedia

Photo: 2019, Matti Blume/Wikimedia

Lighthouse Name	Maiden's Tower (Leander's Tower / Kız Kulesi)
Location	Istanbul, Türkiye
Height	23 m (current tower)
Year Built	Original structure: 4th century BCE – Reconstructions: 1110, 1763, 1998
Range	N/A (not a modern navigational lighthouse)
Type	Stone and masonry tower – octagonal dome
Key Features	Romantic and legendary symbol of Istanbul – located mid-Bosphorus
Accessibility	Accessible – restaurant, café, and observation terrace

Salacak, 34668
Üsküdar/İstanbul, Turkey

22C3+CJ Scutari, Istanbul,
Turkey

Leander's Tower
Videos and documentaries

In the beating heart of the Bosphorus, perched on a small islet between Europe and Asia, stands one of the most evocative and beloved towers of the Eastern Mediterranean: the Maiden's Tower—known in Turkish as Kız Kulesi, and in the West as Leander's Tower. More a symbolic monument than a true navigational lighthouse, it lives at the crossroads of legend, architecture, and poetry. Its origins date back to antiquity, with some sources claiming a structure stood here as early as the 4th century BCE, during the Greek era. Over the centuries, the tower has served many roles: fortress, customs station, prison, watchtower—and, at times, a lighthouse, though never with the function of a modern beacon. The current structure was rebuilt during the Ottoman period in 1763 and has undergone several restorations, most recently in 1998 and again in 2023.

The name "Maiden's Tower" comes from several legends, the most famous telling of an emperor who confined his daughter there to protect her from a fatal prophecy. But fate proved stronger than walls: the maiden ultimately died from a snakebite—hidden in a fruit basket. Thus was born the myth of the tragic girl of the Bosphorus, a symbolic sentinel between the waters.

Today, the tower is one of Istanbul's most iconic and romantic landmarks. Accessible only by boat, it houses a restaurant, café, and panoramic terrace, offering sweeping views of the historic cityscape—the Topkapi Palace, the Blue Mosque, and the Asian shoreline—all in one glance. While it no longer serves as a lighthouse, the Maiden's Tower still casts its light across memory and imagination, a timeless sentinel between two continents.

Photo: 2012, Coşkun Kuruderviş/Wikimedia

United Kingdom – Bell Rock Lighthouse

Source: Google

Photo: 2013, Kognos/Wikimedia

Lighthouse Name	Bell Rock Lighthouse
Location	Arbroath, Angus, Scotland (United Kingdom)
Height	35 m
Year Built	1811
Range	18 nautical miles (approx. 33 km)
Type	Stone tower on submerged reef – automated light
Key Features	Oldest operating offshore lighthouse in the world
Accessibility	Not accessible – visible only by sea or helicopter

Arbroath, Angus, Scotland, United Kingdom

56°25'17"N 2°23'19"W

Bell Rock Lighthouse Videos and documentaries

Carved between waves and legend, the Bell Rock Lighthouse is the oldest offshore lighthouse still in operation anywhere in the world—and one of the greatest feats of British civil engineering. It stands atop a treacherous submerged reef about 18 kilometers off the coast of Arbroath, on Scotland's eastern shore, and takes its name from the Bell Rock, which—according to medieval lore—was once marked by a bell installed by monks… later stolen by a pirate and swallowed by the sea.

Built between 1807 and 1811, the lighthouse was designed by renowned engineer Robert Stevenson, grandfather of Treasure Island author Robert Louis Stevenson. The construction was a legendary endeavor: the rock was exposed only a few hours a day at low tide, and workers operated from platforms suspended over the ocean, facing relentless storms and fierce conditions. The tower was constructed entirely from interlocking stone blocks, laid without mortar, with such precision that it still impresses engineers today.

Standing 35 meters tall, the structure has withstood more than two centuries of tempests and has been fully automated since 1988. Its light, with a range of 18 nautical miles, continues to watch over one of the most dangerous stretches of Scotland's coast, notorious for shipwrecks and hidden reefs.

Inaccessible to the public, Bell Rock can only be seen from the sea or air, yet it remains an icon of maritime heritage and technological history. Historians have called it "the perfect lighthouse," for both its design and enduring strength. Today, it is more than a beacon—it is a monument to human ingenuity, built where no man was thought able to tread. A lighthouse that defies time, the sea, and oblivion.

Photo: 2013, Sandy Gerrard/Wikimedia

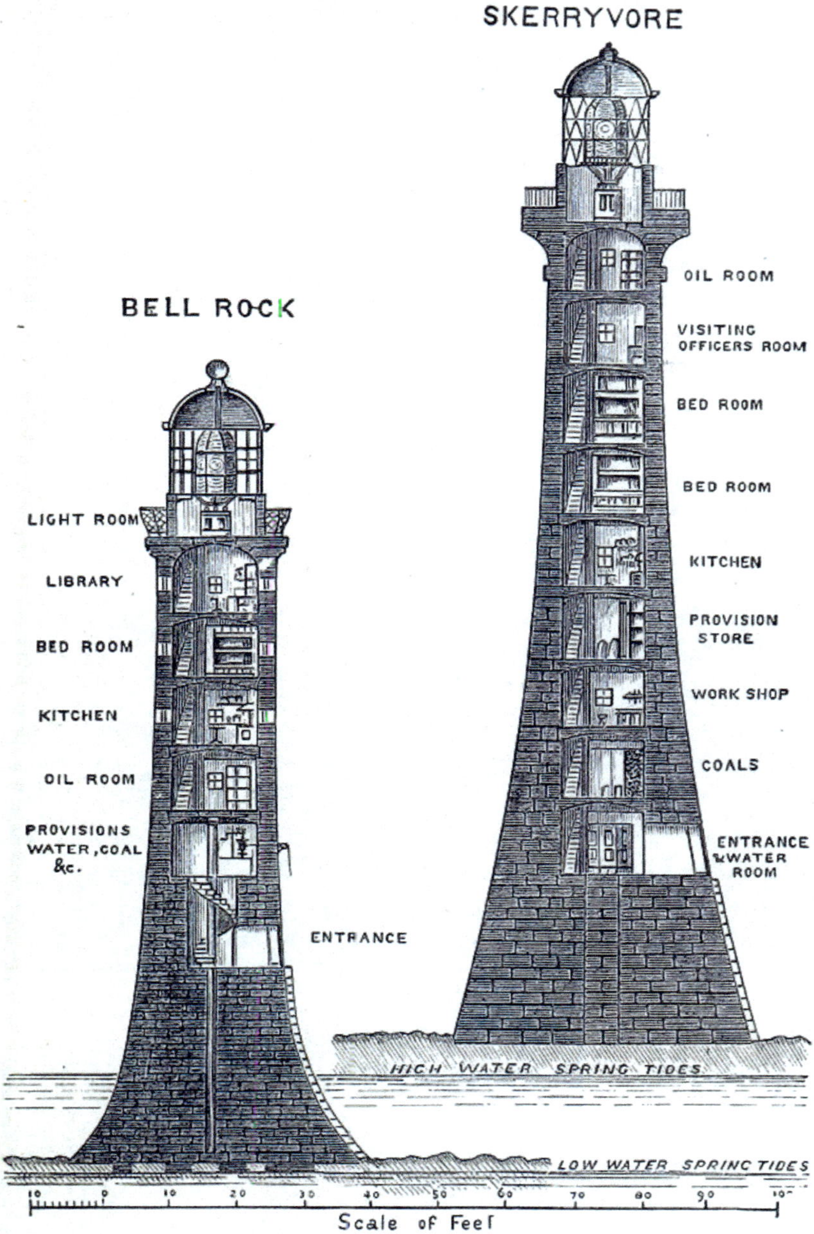

SECTIONS OF BELL ROCK AND SKERRYVORE LIGHTHOUSES.

E.P. Edwards, *Our seamarks*, 1884

United Kingdom – Eddystone Lighthouse

Source: Google

Photo: 2015, Nilfanion/Wikimedia

Vilhelm Melbye (1824-1882), *Shipping off the Eddystone Lighthouse* – Sotheby's

Lighthouse Name	Eddystone Lighthouse
Location	Devon (off the coast of Plymouth), England, United Kingdom
Height	49 m
Year Built	1882 (current tower, fourth version)
Range	17 nautical miles (approx. 31 km)
Type	Granite tower – automated optics
Key Features	First lighthouse ever built on an offshore reef – icon of lighthouse engineering
Accessibility	Not open to the public – accessible only by sea for special visits

Eddystone Lighthouse, United Kingdom

50°13'39"N 4°16'14"W

Eddystone Lighthouse Videos and documentaries

No lighthouse has a story as turbulent and symbolic as that of the Eddystone, perched on a group of dangerous rocks about 14 nautical miles off the coast of Plymouth, in the English Channel. It was here, in the 17th century, that the modern concept of an offshore lighthouse was born: a permanent structure capable of withstanding the fury of the open sea.

The first lighthouse was built in 1698 by Henry Winstanley, who perished along with his creation during a devastating storm in 1703. A series of reconstructions followed, each more advanced than the last: the second tower collapsed, while the third—designed by John Smeaton in 1759—became an engineering landmark, with its iconic "truncated cone" shape that inspired countless lighthouses around the world.

The current tower, constructed in 1882 by James Douglass, is the fourth and final version: 49 meters tall and anchored into solid granite. Its light is now fully automated, yet the tower remains a symbol of the enduring battle between human ingenuity and the forces of nature.

The Eddystone Lighthouse marked a turning point in maritime history. Although not freely accessible, its distinctive black-and-white stripes and remote location in the gray English sea continue to captivate sailors, engineers, and artists alike.

For anyone fascinated by lighthouses, Eddystone is unavoidable: the original stone on which all ocean lighthouses were built.

Photo: 2012, Steve Fareham/Wikimedia

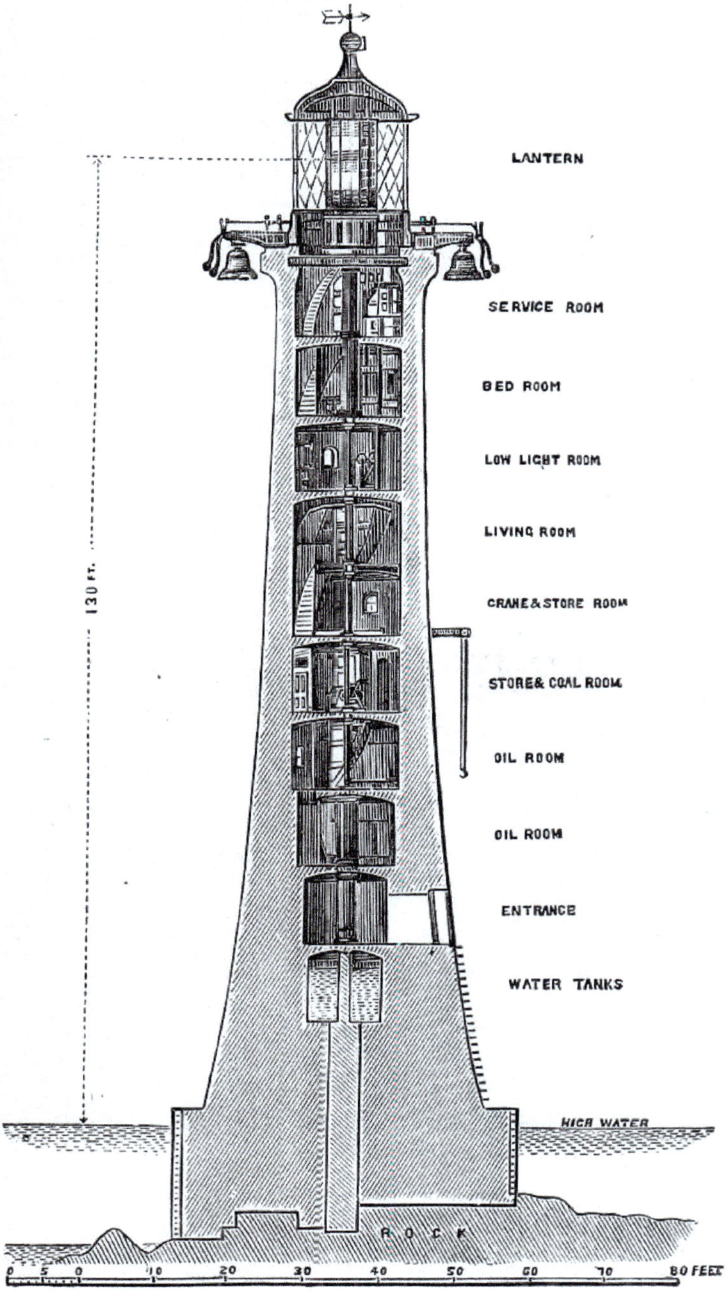

SECTION OF NEW EDDYSTONE LIGHTHOUSE.

E.P. Edwards, *Our seamarks*, 1884

United Kingdom – Low Lighthouse

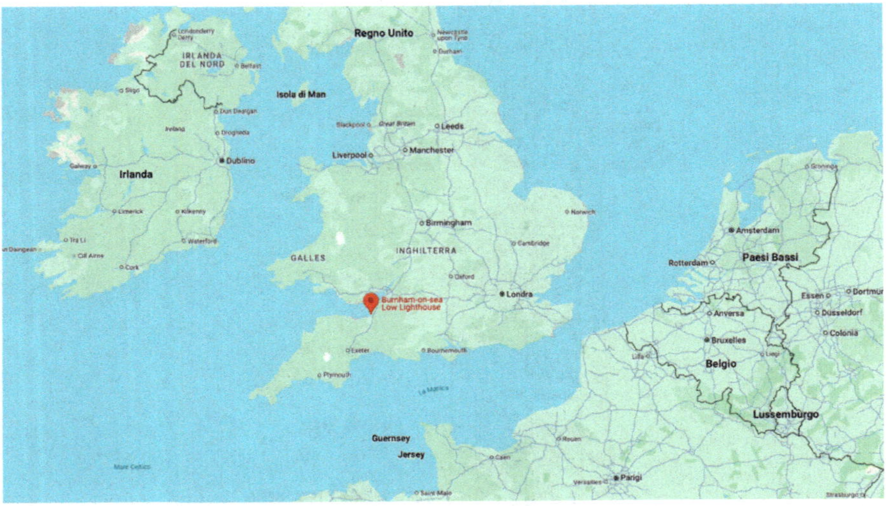

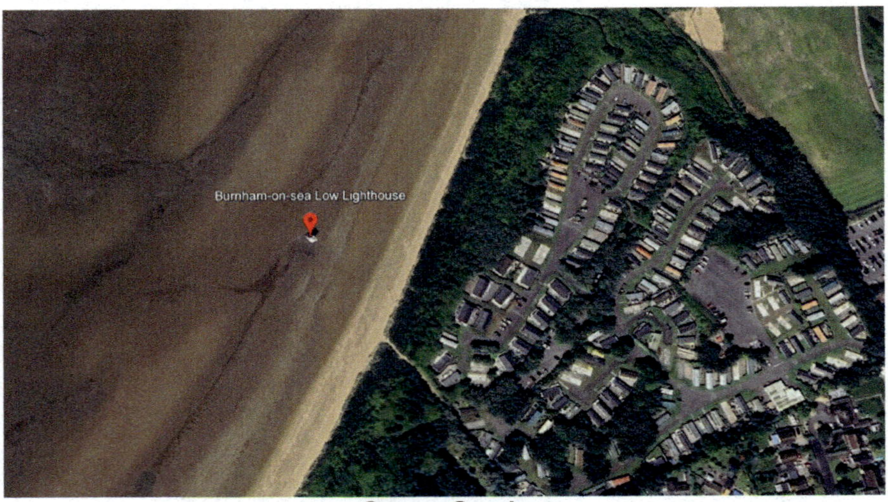

Source: Google

Lighthouse Name	Low Lighthouse
Location	Burnham-on-Sea, England – United Kingdom
Height	9 m
Year Built	1832
Range	11 nautical miles (approx. 20 km)
Type	Wooden structure on nine stilts, white square tower with a red vertical stripe
Key Features	One-of-a-kind "lighthouse on legs," visible at low tide
Accessibility	Accessible from the beach (exterior only); not open to the public

River Parrett, United Kingdom

6XXV+9M Burnham-on-Sea, United Kingdom

Low Lighthouse
Videos and documentaries

It looks like something out of a fairytale or a surrealist film—but it's very real: Burnham-on-Sea's Low Lighthouse, also known as the "Lighthouse on Legs," is one of the most unique structures in the entire history of maritime navigation. Built in 1832 on the sands of Somerset's coast, this white wooden lighthouse—raised on nine long dark stilts—is a masterpiece of adaptive engineering. The Burnham-on-Sea area is known for having some of the highest tidal ranges in the world, with muddy and sandy seabeds that constantly shift. To prevent the beacon from being submerged or damaged, engineers designed this elevated tower, with an external staircase and a lantern mounted atop its square structure, easily recognizable thanks to a bold vertical red stripe painted on one side. At just 9 meters tall, it's one of the shortest lighthouses featured in this volume—but undoubtedly one of the most captivating. Active until the 1960s, the lighthouse was later decommissioned and eventually restored. Though it no longer serves a navigational function, it has become a visual icon of the town and a popular destination for photographers—especially at sunrise or sunset, when the tides either engulf or isolate it entirely.

The Low Lighthouse is a celebration of form born from function—a structure that challenges traditional lighthouse design and proves that utility can give rise to a new, minimal yet unforgettable aesthetic

Photo: 2017, MichaelMaggs/Wikimedia

Photo: 2008, IDS.photos/Wikimedia

United Kingdom – Neist Point Lighthouse

Source: Google

Photo: 2013, JoachimKohler-HB/Wikimedia

Lighthouse Name	Neist Point Lighthouse
Location	Isle of Skye, Scotland, United Kingdom
Height	19 m (tower) – 43 m above sea level (focal height)
Year Built	1909
Range	16 nautical miles (approx. 30 km)
Type	White square tower with black lantern – reinforced concrete construction
Key Features	Remote lighthouse in one of Scotland's most scenic coastal spots
Accessibility	Not open to the public – exterior accessible via panoramic walking path

Isle of Skye IV55 8WU, United Kingdom

C6F6+9M Waterstein, Isle of Skye, United Kingdom

Neist Point Lighthouse Videos and documentaries

On the western edge of the Isle of Skye, perched on a dark cliff jutting out into the Atlantic like a solitary promontory, stands Neist Point Lighthouse—one of the most iconic images of wild, windswept Scotland. The road to get there is long and winding, ending in a narrow path high above the sea, where every step is accompanied only by the sound of wind and waves.

The lighthouse was built in 1909, designed by David Alan Stevenson—a member of the famed Scottish family of engineers responsible for dozens of lighthouses along the British coastline. The compact white square tower is made of reinforced concrete and is flanked by several service buildings, now abandoned.

Though not among the tallest or most advanced beacons, Neist Point is famous for its dramatic setting. From here, the panoramic view sweeps across the Atlantic Ocean, the Outer Hebrides, and—on lucky days—even dolphins playing in the surf. It's one of the best places on the island to watch the sunset or, in colder months, catch a glimpse of the northern lights.

The interior is not open to visitors, but the scenic path leading to the lighthouse is one of Scotland's most photographed walks. Those who reach the end rarely forget the feeling of standing at the edge of the world—where man's light meets the vastness of nature.

Photo: 2014, Lionel Ulmer/Wikimedia

United Kingdom – Skerryvore Lighthouse

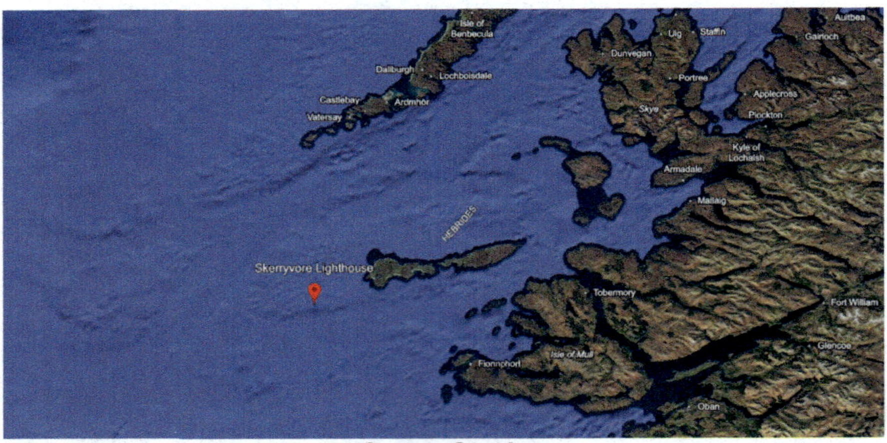

Source: Google

Lighthouse Name	Skerryvore Lighthouse
Location	Off the coast of Tiree, Inner Hebrides, Scotland, UK
Height	48 m
Year Built	1844
Range	20 nautical miles (approx. 37 km)
Type	Granite tower – engineering masterpiece by Alan Stevenson
Key Features	Regarded as the most beautiful and inaccessible lighthouse in the UK
Accessibility	Not open to the public – accessible only by sea, extremely hard to approach

Skerryvore Lighthouse, United Kingdom

56°22'01"N 7°09'40"W

Skerryvore Lighthouse Videos and documentaries

Perched on a submerged reef in the Atlantic Ocean, 18 kilometers off the Isle of Tiree, Skerryvore Lighthouse rises like a monument to human courage and perseverance in the face of the sea's fury. Standing 48 meters tall, it is the tallest lighthouse in Scotland and one of the most revered feats of engineering in the world of maritime navigation.

It was built between 1838 and 1844 by Alan Stevenson, a member of the renowned Scottish lighthouse-building dynasty and cousin to novelist Robert Louis Stevenson. The challenges were immense: freezing winds, relentless storms, and the need for a specially built support base on the nearby island of Hynish to carry out the work. The result was a massive granite tower, masterfully crafted to withstand the full force of the ocean for decades.

Remote, solitary, and notoriously difficult to reach, Skerryvore has been fully automated since 1994. Its architectural elegance and engineering daring have led many to describe it as "the most beautiful lighthouse in Britain." Over the years, it has inspired artists, writers, and engineers across the globe.

Although it cannot be visited, Skerryvore remains one of the most captivating lighthouses on the planet—a stone column rising from the deep, challenging the elements and guiding sailors through the treacherous waters of the Hebrides for nearly two centuries.

Photo: 2021, Rob Farrow/Wikimedia

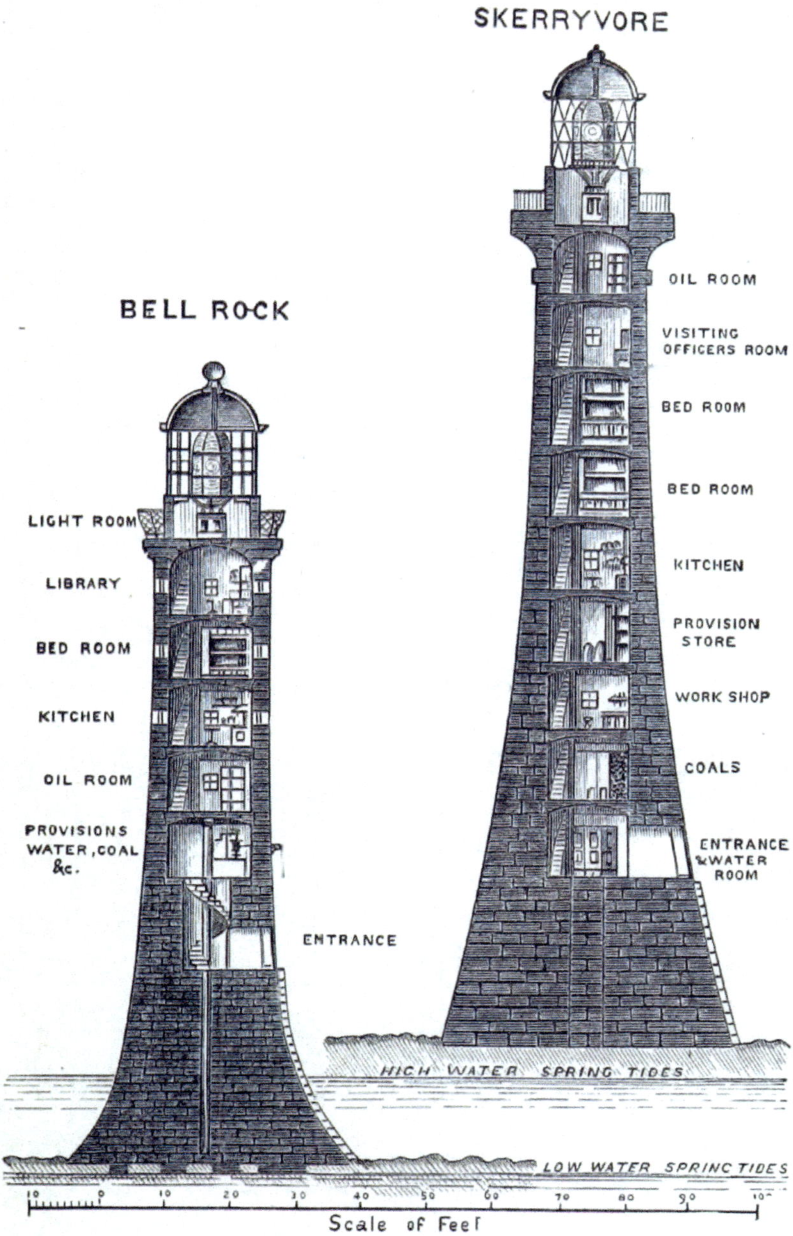

SECTIONS OF BELL ROCK AND SKERRYVORE LIGHTHOUSES.

E.P. Edwards, *Our seamarks*, 1884

United Kingdom – Souter Lighthouse

Source: Google

Photo: 2010, Malcolm Tebbit/Wikimedia

Lighthouse Name	Souter Lighthouse
Location	South Shields, Tyne and Wear, England
Height	23 m
Year Built	1871
Range	26 nautical miles (approx. 48 km)
Type	Cylindrical white masonry tower with red bands – electric-powered
Key Features	World's first lighthouse purpose-built to operate on electricity
Accessibility	Accessible – museum and scenic viewpoint (managed by the National Trust)

Coast Rd, Whitburn, Sunderland SR6 7NH, United Kingdom

XJCP+69 Sunderland, United Kingdom

Souter Lighthouse Videos and documentaries

Perched atop the high cliffs of England's northeastern coast, between Sunderland and South Shields, Souter Lighthouse stands as a symbol of the Industrial Revolution and the advent of modern maritime technology. Opened in 1871, it was the world's first lighthouse specifically designed and constructed to run entirely on electricity—a groundbreaking innovation at the time.

Its distinctive white-and-red-banded tower dominates the North Sea landscape in the area known as Whitburn, a notoriously dangerous stretch of coastline littered with shipwrecks. The original lighting system, powered by dynamos and steam engines, produced a rotating beam visible for more than 25 nautical miles—a true marvel of Victorian engineering.

Although only 23 meters tall, the lighthouse sits atop elevated cliffs, giving it outstanding visibility. It remained operational until 1988, when it was decommissioned and entrusted to the National Trust, which transformed it into a museum. Today, Souter Lighthouse is fully open to the public: visitors can explore the tower, the keepers' quarters, the original machinery, and the massive Fresnel lens. The view from the top offers a spectacular panorama of the North Sea horizon.

Each year, the site welcomes thousands of visitors with exhibitions, educational programs, and interactive displays. Souter is more than a lighthouse—it's a beacon of human innovation, maritime safety, and British ingenuity in blending technological progress with natural beauty.

Photo: 2017, Tim Withnall/Wikimedia

United States – Boston Light

Source: Google

Photo: 2010, Doc Searls/Wikimedia

Photo: 2013, Robert Linsdell/Wikimedia

Lighthouse Name	Boston Light
Location	Little Brewster Island, Boston Harbor, Massachusetts, United States
Height	28 m (tower height) – 33 m above sea level (focal height)
Year Built	1716 (current tower: 1783)
Range	27 nautical miles (approx. 50 km)
Type	White conical masonry tower – automated light with resident keeper
Key Features	First lighthouse built in the United States – only one still staffed by a civilian keeper
Accessibility	Seasonally accessible – reachable only by boat

Little Brewster Island, Boston, MA, USA

84H5+5W Boston, Massachusetts, USA

Boston Light
Videos and documentaries

In the heart of American history and on the calm waters of Boston Harbor stands Boston Light, the first lighthouse ever built in the United States and still active today. It dates back to 1716, when the British colonies decided to construct a beacon to mark the entrance to New England's most important port. The original tower was destroyed during the Revolutionary War, and the current 28-meter structure was rebuilt in 1783.

Despite the light now being fully automated, Boston Light remains the only lighthouse in the country still staffed by a civilian keeper—a tradition preserved for its symbolic and historical significance. Its beam, visible up to 27 nautical miles, continues to guide ships into the harbor alongside modern radar and sound signals.

Perched on the small, rocky Little Brewster Island, Boston Light is jointly managed by the National Park Service and the U.S. Coast Guard. Access is only possible by sea, and guided tours are offered during the summer months, including climbs to the lantern and visits to the keeper's quarters.

Boston Light is more than just a lighthouse: it is America's original beacon—an enduring symbol of independence, maritime heritage, and the unbroken line between past and present.

Photo: 2008, Hull/Wikimedia

United States – Cape Hatteras Light

Source: Google

Photo: 2017, Scott0650/Wikimedia

Lighthouse Name	Cape Hatteras Light
Location	Buxton, Outer Banks, North Carolina, USA
Height	63 m (tower height) – 63 m above sea level (focal height)
Year Built	1870 (reconstruction)
Range	24 nautical miles (approx. 44 km)
Type	Conical brick tower – black and white spiral stripes
Key Features	Tallest brick lighthouse in the United States – symbol of the Outer Banks
Accessibility	Accessible – open seasonally for tower climbs

46379 Lighthouse Rd, Buxton, NC 27920, USA	7F2C+6F Buxton, North Carolina, USA	Cape Hatteras Light Videos and documentaries

Rising from the windswept dunes and stormy shores of North Carolina's Outer Banks, Cape Hatteras Light stands as the tallest brick lighthouse in the United States—and one of the tallest in the world. Its iconic black-and-white spiral stripes have made it a symbol of coastal engineering and a powerful emblem of where wild nature meets human resilience.

The current tower, completed in 1870, replaced an earlier structure built in 1803, which proved inadequate for warning ships about the perils of the "Graveyard of the Atlantic"—a treacherous stretch of ocean infamous for shipwrecks caused by shifting sandbars, strong currents, and sudden weather changes.

In 1999, the entire lighthouse was painstakingly dismantled and relocated nearly 900 meters inland to protect it from coastal erosion. This monumental feat is still considered one of the most remarkable preservation efforts ever undertaken on a lighthouse.

Today, Cape Hatteras Light is open seasonally to visitors. Those who climb its 250+ steps are rewarded with breathtaking views of the Atlantic Ocean and the pristine beaches of the Cape Hatteras National Seashore. The lighthouse is managed by the National Park Service, which also oversees the adjacent museum and educational trails.

More than a navigational aid, Cape Hatteras Light is a towering monument to endurance—against time, tides, and the relentless sea. A giant of brick and light, still standing guard over centuries of storms, shipwrecks, and stories.

Photo: 2013, U.S. National Park Service/Wikimedia

United States – Diamond Head Lighthouse

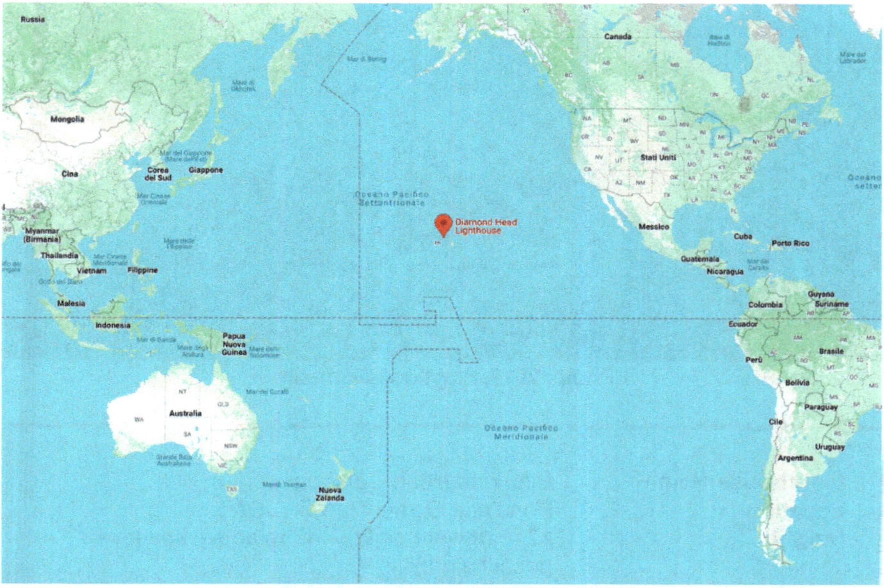

Source: Google

Photo: 2014, Praytino/Wikimedia

Lighthouse Name	Diamond Head Lighthouse
Location	Honolulu, O‘ahu, Hawaii, USA
Height	17 m (tower height) – 45 m above sea level (focal height)
Year Built	1899 (current tower: 1917)
Range	18 nautical miles (approx. 33 km)
Type	White cylindrical concrete tower – automated optic
Key Features	One of the Pacific's most iconic lighthouses – Hawaiian cultural and military landmark
Accessibility	Not open to the public – visible from scenic hiking trail

3399 Diamond Head Rd, Honolulu, HI 96815, USA

754R+76 Honolulu, Hawaii, USA

Diamond Head Lighthouse Videos and documentaries

Set along the southern slope of the Diamond Head volcanic crater, overlooking the endless blue of the Pacific Ocean, Diamond Head Lighthouse is far more than a navigational aid—it's a beloved Hawaiian landmark cherished by both sailors and tourists in Honolulu.

Originally built in 1899 and rebuilt in its current form in 1917, the lighthouse was part of a broader modernization of American naval infrastructure in the Pacific. Its 17-meter white concrete tower, perched about 45 meters above sea level, remains operational to this day, though now fully automated.

While the lighthouse itself is not open to the public, it can be seen from the popular Diamond Head Summit Trail, which offers one of the most iconic views on the island. Managed by the United States Coast Guard, the lighthouse is an enduring symbol on the Waikiki coastline. Over the years, it has appeared in commercials, postcards, travel posters, and even postage stamps—earning its place among America's most beloved beacons.

Surrounded by tropical vegetation, blue waters, and surfers catching waves below, Diamond Head Lighthouse continues to shine—a reminder that even in paradise, a guiding light is essential.

Photo: 2010, TruffShuff/Wikimedia

United States – East Brother Light Station

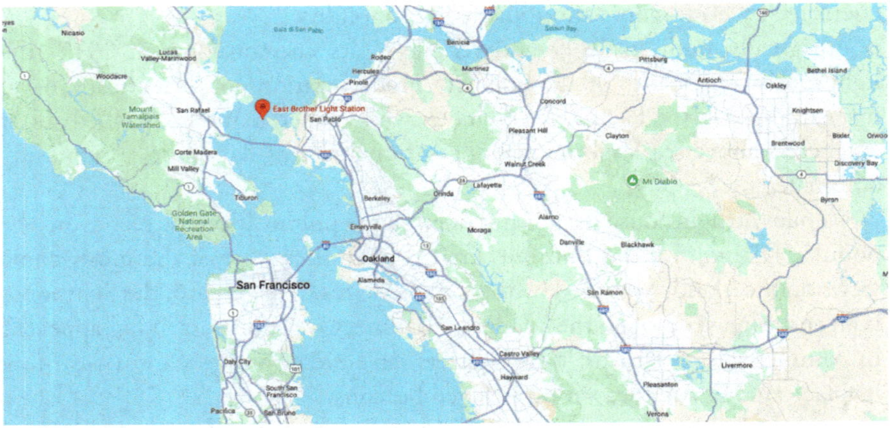

Source: Google

Photo: 2013, Frank Schulenburg/Wikimedia

Photo: 2013, Frank Schulenburg/Wikimedia

Lighthouse Name	East Brother Light Station
Location	San Pablo Bay, Richmond, California, USA
Height	15 m (tower height) – 19 m above sea level (focal height)
Year Built	1874
Range	18 nautical miles (approx. 33 km)
Type	White cast-iron tower atop a Victorian house – automated light
Key Features	Historic lighthouse turned into a bed & breakfast – one of the most unique in the world
Accessibility	Accessible

1900 Stenmark Dr,
Richmond, CA 94801, USA

XH78+8M Richmond,
California, USA

East Brother Lighthouse
Videos and documentaries

On a tiny rocky islet in San Pablo Bay, just north of San Francisco Bay, stands the charming East Brother Light Station: a Victorian-style lighthouse that now doubles as an elegant bed and breakfast perched above the ocean, accessible only by boat. Opened in 1874, it was part of a crucial coastal signaling system guiding maritime traffic to the cities of Richmond, Vallejo, and San Francisco. The lighthouse features a 15-meter white cast-iron tower built atop a picturesque 19th-century keeper's house, complete with wooden trims and red roofs. The residence has been meticulously preserved, offering a glimpse into the original life of lighthouse keepers. After its light was automated in 1969, the station faced abandonment but was saved by a passionate group of local citizens who lovingly restored it. Today, guests can spend the night in the lighthouse, dine in the original dining room, hear the foghorn echo across the waves, and wake up to breathtaking bay views. The experience includes guided tours, short hikes on the island, and moments of complete stillness—far from the buzz of modern life.

While the lighthouse still fulfills its maritime duty, it has become a romantic and historical refuge, a favorite among travelers, lighthouse enthusiasts, and photographers alike. Few places blend vintage architecture, ocean scenery, and timeless hospitality so seamlessly.

East Brother Light Station is a window into the past—and a gateway to a one-of-a-kind experience, where the lighthouse not only lights the sea but warmly welcomes its guests with history, heart, and true light.

United States – Pigeon Point Lighthouse

Source: Google

Photo: 2016, Frank Schulenburg/Wikimedia

Lighthouse Name	Pigeon Point Lighthouse
Location	Pescadero, San Mateo County, California, USA
Height	35 m (tower height) – 48 m above sea level (focal height)
Year Built	1872
Range	24 nautical miles (approx. 44 km)
Type	White cylindrical masonry tower – lantern with Fresnel lens (under restoration)
Key Features	One of the tallest lighthouses in the U.S. – iconic cliffside setting
Accessibility	Accessible – state park, hostel, visitor center

210 Pigeon Point Rd,
Pescadero, CA 94060, USA

5JJ4+M6 Pescadero,
California, USA

Pigeon Point Lighthouse
Videos and documentaries

Perched on the rugged cliffs between Santa Cruz and San Francisco, Pigeon Point Lighthouse stands tall as one of the tallest and most picturesque lighthouses in the United States. First lit in 1872 and rising 35 meters, it was built to mark one of the most treacherous stretches of the Pacific coast—named after the Carrier Pigeon, a shipwrecked vessel that gave the site its name.

Its elegant white tower commands sweeping views of the Pacific Ocean, offering postcard-worthy sunsets and a dramatic backdrop for photography. Originally equipped with a powerful first-order Fresnel lens, the lighthouse now uses a modern light source while the historic lens undergoes careful restoration.

Though automated, the light is still operational, continuing its duty as a coastal beacon. Today, the site is part of the Pigeon Point Light Station State Historic Park, welcoming thousands of visitors annually with its scenic trails, visitor center, and a unique oceanside hostel housed in the former keepers' quarters.

While the tower itself is currently closed to the public due to ongoing structural work, the site remains one of the most photographed on the California coast—an ideal location for spotting migrating whales, seabirds, and experiencing the raw beauty of the West Coast.

Pigeon Point is more than a lighthouse; it's a monument to navigation and natural splendor, where maritime history and Pacific wilderness meet in a landscape of striking simplicity.

Photo: 2009, John Loo/Wikimedia

United States – Point Reyes Lighthouse

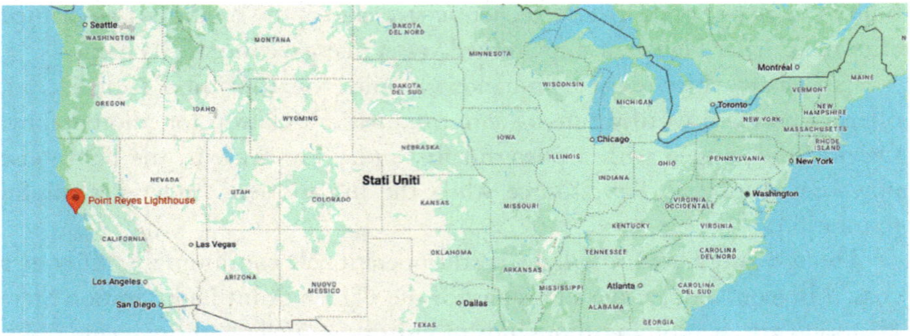

Source: Google

Photo: 2012, Frank Schulenburg/Wikimedia

Lighthouse Name	Point Reyes Lighthouse
Location	Point Reyes, Marin County, California, USA
Height	11 m (tower height) – 88 m above sea level (focal height)
Year Built	1870
Range	24 nautical miles (approx. 44 km)
Type	Octagonal cast-iron tower – lantern with 16 glass panels
Key Features	Historic lighthouse on one of the windiest and foggiest headlands in the U.S.
Accessibility	Accessible – visitor center, panoramic 300-step staircase

Inverness, California
94937, USA

37°59'44"N 123°01'24"W

Point Reyes Lighthouse
Videos and documentaries

Perched atop a steep cliff plunging into the Pacific Ocean, the Point Reyes Lighthouse is one of the most striking and dramatic beacons along the American West Coast. Located about 30 miles (50 km) north of San Francisco, at the heart of the Point Reyes National Seashore, it was built in 1870 to mark a treacherous stretch of coast infamous for thick fog, relentless winds, and shifting currents.

Though the tower itself stands only 11 meters tall, it sits 88 meters above sea level on a sheer rock face, giving its beam exceptional reach—24 nautical miles—thanks to a powerful first-order Fresnel lens. The octagonal cast-iron structure and its 16-pane glass lantern make it a textbook example of 19th-century American lighthouse design.

Point Reyes is notable for its dramatic isolation. To reach it, visitors must follow a scenic trail and descend a staircase of over 300 steps carved into the cliffside—an effort rewarded by sweeping views of the endless Pacific, often shrouded in fog or echoing with the roar of the wind.

Decommissioned in 1975 and now automated, the lighthouse is part of the National Park Service's visitor facilities and remains a popular destination for hikers, photographers, and nature lovers. During certain seasons, it's also a prime spot for observing migrating gray whales from its panoramic terraces.

Point Reyes Lighthouse is more than a beacon—it's a breathtaking, almost spiritual encounter with the edge of the continent. A place where land, sea, and imagination meet on the wind-swept cliffs of northern California.

Photo: 2007, Eric Chan/Wikimedia

United States – Portland Head Light

Source: Google

Photo: 2009, Rapidfire/Wikimedia

Lighthouse Name	Portland Head Light
Location	Cape Elizabeth, Portland, Maine, USA
Height	24 m (tower height) – 31 m above sea level (focal height)
Year Built	1791
Range	24 nautical miles (approx. 44 km)
Type	White conical masonry tower with black lantern – automated light
Key Features	One of the most photographed and oldest lighthouses in the USA
Accessibility	Accessible – museum, park, and scenic walking trails i

Cape Elizabeth, ME 04107, USA

JQFR+6R Cape Elizabeth, Maine, USA

Portland Head Light Videos and documentaries

Perched atop a rocky promontory overlooking the Atlantic Ocean, Portland Head Light is one of the most iconic, photographed, and beloved lighthouses in the United States. Located in Cape Elizabeth, Maine, it is the oldest lighthouse in New England still in operation, first lit in 1791 by direct order of George Washington.

Built as a white masonry tower with a distinctive black lantern, the 24-meter-tall structure has guided vessels into Portland Harbor for centuries, guarding a treacherous coastline known for hidden rocks and sudden fog. Automated in 1989, the lighthouse remains fully operational today, while the historic keeper's house now serves as a museum that traces the maritime history of the Maine coast.

Surrounding the lighthouse is Fort Williams Park, a public space offering panoramic trails, open green areas, and spectacular viewpoints overlooking the ocean. It's not uncommon to see painters at their easels, professional photographers with tripods, and visitors from around the world, all drawn to the timeless charm of Portland Head Light. Every element—from the crashing waves below the cliff to the shifting colors of the sky across the seasons—adds to its status as a quintessential American lighthouse.

Even in an age of satellites and digital navigation, Portland Head Light continues to shine in the collective imagination. It's more than a beacon—it's a living postcard, a piece of America etched in rock, sea, and memory.

Photo: 2009, N.V. Deremer/Wikimedia

United States – Split Rock Lighthouse

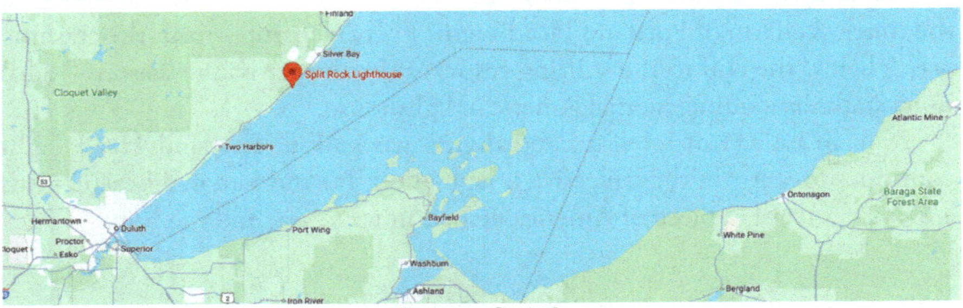

Source: Google

Photo: 2009, Jim Sorbie/Wikimedia

Photo: 2014, Dougtone/Wikimedia

Lighthouse Name	Split Rock Lighthouse
Location	Two Harbors, Minnesota, USA
Height	17 m
Year Built	1910
Range	22 nautical miles (approx. 41 km)
Type	Octagonal concrete tower – third-order Fresnel lens
Key Features	One of the world's most scenic inland lighthouses, perched on a cliff above Lake Superior
Accessibility	Open to the public – part of a State Historic Park, museum accessible

3713 Split Rock Lighthouse Rd, Two Harbors, MN 55616, USA

5JXM+X5 Two Harbors, Minnesota, USA

Split Rock Lighthouse Videos and documentaries

In the heart of Minnesota, overlooking a remote and breathtaking stretch of Lake Superior, stands one of the most iconic and photographed lighthouses in the United States: Split Rock Lighthouse. Perched atop a 40-meter-high cliff of volcanic rock, it rises like a solitary castle suspended above the water.

Built in 1910, the lighthouse was commissioned after a devastating storm in 1905 that sank 29 ships on the lake. In response, the federal government launched one of the most advanced engineering projects of the era. The octagonal tower was constructed from reinforced concrete and equipped with a third-order Fresnel lens imported from France.

Thanks to its dramatic location and its North American rustic architectural style, Split Rock has become a pilgrimage site for lighthouse enthusiasts, photographers, and travelers alike. Although it was decommissioned as an official aid to navigation in 1969, the lighthouse has been impeccably preserved and transformed into a museum. Each year on November 10, its light is ceremonially lit in honor of the lives lost in the sinking of the Edmund Fitzgerald, one of the most famous shipwrecks in Great Lakes history.

Today, Split Rock stands as a symbol of the northern American frontier, the power of nature, and the serene beauty of freshwater landscapes. Though inland, this lighthouse possesses the grandeur and presence of its ocean-bound counterparts.

Photo: 2007, Tony Webster/Wikimedia

United States – St. Joseph Lighthouse

Fonti: Google

Photo: 2014, Rachel Kramer/Wikimedia

Lighthouse Name	St. Joseph Lighthouse
Location	St. Joseph, Michigan, USA
Height	11 m (front light) – 17 m (rear light)
Year Built	1906 (original lighthouse from 1832)
Range	20 nautical miles (approx. 37 km)
Type	Metal cylindrical tower with octagonal lantern on pier catwalk – automated light
Key Features	Famous for its dramatic winter ice formations – symbol of Lake Michigan
Accessibility	Open to the public only externally – visible from the beach and pier

80 Ridgeway St, St Joseph, MI 49085, USA

4G77+WV St. Joseph, Michigan, USA

St. Joseph Lighthouse Videos and documentaries

Few lighthouses capture the raw beauty of the American winter like the St. Joseph Lighthouse, located at the end of the pier in St. Joseph, Michigan, overlooking the vast expanse of Lake Michigan. It is renowned not only for its navigational role but also for the haunting images that go viral each winter: the tower encased in thick ice, transformed into a surreal natural sculpture, balanced between beauty and danger.

The first light station at this site was established in 1832, but the current structure dates to 1906. It consists of two aligned lights connected by an elevated catwalk, originally designed to allow keepers to access the lantern even during violent storms. The rear light—the taller of the two—features a cylindrical metal tower topped by a white and red cupola and remains operational today.

Throughout the 20th century, the St. Joseph Lighthouse has become both a symbol of Great Lakes navigation and a favorite subject for nature photographers, especially in the colder months when waves and Arctic storms turn it into a fleeting masterpiece.

Now automated, the lighthouse is only accessible externally, via a pier walkway that extends from the town center. The contrast between the delicate beam of light and the immense power of the lake makes St. Joseph a unique beacon, telling the everyday epic of America's inland shores through ice, wind, and fog.

Photo: 2008, C. Landis/Wikimedia

Legal Notice

Photo Credits

All images published in this volume are used in compliance with applicable copyright laws, including Italian Law No. 633 of 1941 (as amended) and the Berne Convention for the Protection of Literary and Artistic Works. Most of the reproduced images fall into one of the following categories:

• Images sourced from Wikimedia Commons, used in accordance with the applicable Creative Commons licenses (e.g., CC BY, CC BY-SA, CC0); when required, author and source have been credited.

• Simple or purely documentary photographs in the public domain under Italian copyright law (Articles 87 ff., Law No. 633/1941), due to their age (over 20 years) and lack of creative originality.

• Low-resolution reproductions of works in the public domain.

• Images used for purposes of research, criticism, commentary, illustration, or education, as part of a scholarly work, in accordance with Article 70 of Italian Copyright Law No. 633/1941.

The Author and Publisher assume no liability for any misuse of the images contained in this volume by third parties.

Every effort has been made to identify image authors and provide accurate credit. In the event of any errors or omissions, the Author and Publisher will be glad to make corrections or additions in future editions.

QR Codes and Online Content

All QR codes included in this volume link to publicly accessible online content as of the publication date. However, the Author and Publisher cannot guarantee the continued availability, accuracy, or legal status of third-party materials linked via QR codes.

The Author and Publisher disclaim any responsibility for changes, removals, or alterations to linked web addresses occurring after this book was printed.

Visio Series

Visual Explorations
Art, architecture, fashion, cinema, and visual culture

Discover all our titles:

Il Disoriente
Great classics of fiction

Astra
Essays and stories beyond Earth

Brěvitěr
Legal manuals and compendiums

Crimina
Crime & Noir

First English Books
The finest literary classics for English learners

Focus Tematici
Close to, inside, and beyond things

I Grandi della Letteratura
Masterpieces in 6×9 format
with high-legibility text

Imaginaria
Science Fiction • Fantasy • Adventure

Mille Bolle Blu
Books for children

Mysteria
Mystery fiction and essays

Politicamente
Political essays and writings

Retoricamente
Rhetoric, language, and communication

Saggiamente
Essays in the humanities and social sciences

Teatro da leggere
Plays to read

Università
Essays and textbooks

Visio
Visual explorations

Printed in Dunstable, United Kingdom

71372699R00097